"This volume is a wonderful practical resource for training others in orthodox confessional doctrine. Its extensive use of Scripture roots it firmly in the Word of God, and its engaging inductive method elicits active learning from the student. This curriculum will be useful both in churches and homes for training not only younger people, but also adults, helping to form their minds in good biblical teaching and exhorting their hearts to rejoice in the great God of truth."

Tom Hicks
Pastor of First Baptist Church, Clinton, LA

"This study guide by Jimmy Johnson gives to churches a highly useful tool for learning Scripture, doctrine, and personal growth in grace through truth. The combination of the questions from the Baptist Catechism, the corresponding chapters from the *Second London Confession*, and the Scripture proofs gives opportunity for pertinent questions concerning the meaning of Scripture and grasping of doctrinal truth. This will be an effective tool for both instruction in righteousness and contending earnestly for the faith once delivered to the saints."

Tom J. Nettles
Senior Professor of Historical Theology of The Southern Baptist Theological Seminary

"There are many aspects of discipleship but this curriculum focuses on the foundational substance of discipleship. There is no discipleship if God's word is not taught properly. There is no discipleship if God's word is not challenging us to live God honoring lives. There is no discipleship if there is not a strong encouragement in affection for our Lord. This curriculum encourages all three heathy aspects of discipleship: orthodoxy, orthopraxy and orthopathy."

Creston Thomas
Pastor of Christ the Redeemer Church, Pine Bluff, AR

"One of the great needs of our day is a return to the time-honoured method of discipleship through catechetical instruction. The Ancient Church developed such as it moved out from its Jewish matrix into the Gentile world of paganism. Leaders in that day rightly recognized that new converts needed such grounding to make sense of what they had committed themselves to. So catechism preceded baptism. And down through the centuries catechizing became a key element of disciple-making. There is no doubt in my mind that the present-day loss of any basic understanding of the meta-narrative of the Christian Faith in the West necessitates some renewed vehicle of catechism. So I am thrilled by this skilfull adaptation of the Second London Confession of Faith and the traditional Baptist Catechism. Pick up and use it in your families and churches!"

Michael A.G. Haykin,
Chair & Professor of Church History of The Southern Baptist Theological Seminary

Confessing Sound Words

Jimmy Johnson

To Vista Baptist Church of Osceola

JIMMY JOHNSON

CONFESSING SOUND WORDS

A Curriculum through the Second London Baptist Confession of Faith

Confessing Sound Words

Copyright © 2024 Jimmy Johnson

All rights reserved. This book may not be reproduced, in whole or in part, without written permission from the publishers.

Unless otherwise indicated, all Scripture quotations are from The ESV® Bible (The Holy Bible, English Standard Version®), copyright © 2001 by Crossway, a publishing ministry of Good News Publishers. Used by permission. All rights reserved.

H&E Publishing, West Lorne, Ontario
www.hesedandemet.com

Cover design by Chance Faulkner
Interior font: Equity Text A

Paperback ISBN: 978-1-77484-137-2
eBook ISBN: 978-1-77484-138-9

Contents

Foreword xi
Sam Waldron
Introduction 1
Preface 11
To the Judicious and Impartial Reader 11

Chapter 1
   The Holy Scriptures 19

Chapter 2
   Of God and of the Holy Trinity 27

Chapter 3
   Of God's Decree 35

Chapter 4
   Of Creation 41

Chapter 5
   Of Divine Providence 47

Chapter 6
   Of the Fall of Man, of Sin, and of the Punishment Thereof 55

Chapter 7
   Of God's Covenant 63

Chapter 8
   Of Christ the Mediator 69

Chapter 9
   Of Free Will 79

Chapter 10
   Of Effectual Calling 85

Chapter 11
   Of Justification 91

Chapter 12
   Of Adoption 97

Chapter 13
   Of Sanctification 103

Chapter 14
   Of Saving Faith 109

Chapter 15
   Of Repentance Unto Life and Salvation 115

Chapter 16
   Of Good Works 121

Chapter 17
    Of the Perseverance of the Saints 127
Chapter 18
    Of the Assurance of Grace and Salvation...133
Chapter 19
    Of the Law of God 139
Chapter 20
    Of the Gospel and of the Extent of the Grace Thereof 147
Chapter 21
    Of Christian Liberty and Liberty of Conscience...153
Chapter 22
    Of Religious Worship and the Sabbath Day 159
Chapter 23
    Of Lawful Oaths and Vows 167
Chapter 24
    Of the Civil Magistrate 171
Chapter 25
    Of Marriage..177
Chapter 26
    Of the Church 183
Chapter 27
    Of the Communion of the Saints...193
Chapter 28
    Of Baptism and the Lord's Supper...199
Chapter 29
    Of Baptism.. 205
Chapter 30
    Of the Lord's Supper..211
Chapter 31
    Of the State of Man after Death and Of the Resurrection of the Dead 219
Chapter 32
    Of the Last Judgement.. 227
Ending Statement, Signatories, and Appendix on Baptism 233

Acknowledgements... 247
Bibliography 249
Scripture Index...251

Foreword

To many modern Christians, confessionalism may seem strange. After all, they have been told, we have the Bible. Why would we need anything else?

However, it is often also the case that these same modern Christians don't understand their Bibles, even if they read them regularly. They have been implicitly taught to view their Bibles as containing many seemingly unrelated stories whose only connective tissue is some vague relation to God.

Good creeds and confessions are valuable precisely because they reflect and summarize biblical teaching in a clear manner. I firmly believe the Second London Baptist Confession of 1689 (the 1689, in shorthand) to be the most biblical, and therefore most valuable, of these historic Protestant confessions. That is why I wrote *A Modern Exposition of the 1689 Baptist Confession of Faith* 32 years ago, on the 300th anniversary of its original wide publication. The 1689 has served the Baptist church well these past 300 plus years. I rejoice greatly at its modern rediscovery!

You will find in this book a helpful starting point to introduce yourself and your church to the 1689 and the Baptist Catechism. Jimmy Johnson does a wonderful job of guiding you through the confession, chapter by chapter. I am confident that, as you work through this study, you too will see the value in the 1689 and the Baptist Catechism as helpful and accurate summaries of God's revelation to his church, the Bible.

May the Lord greatly bless this study and use it to continue to shape you into the image of his blessed Son, Jesus Christ!

Dr. Sam Waldron
Owensboro, KY
November, 2021

Introduction

The purpose of this curriculum

Before signing to publish the work in your hands, I was writing it for use in the church I pastor. I have been privileged to take two men of my church through several chapters. By doing it this way, I ensure the work is practical. Being practical is key to achieving my purpose in writing it: to equip the saints with the truths of God's Word, reform churches, retrieve Baptist Confessional heritage, and glorify God. As these two men and I have worked through this curriculum, I've seen them encounter God in his Word and converse with the framers of the Second London Baptist Confession of Faith (2LBCF) and the Baptist Catechism (BC).

While working on this project, I was asked and thought to myself, "Why use historic confessions and catechisms for the basis of a discipleship curriculum?" To answer this question, I will define confessions and catechisms, give reasons for their use for discipleship, and provide some benefits of using them for discipleship.

Confessions and catechisms defined

To begin with, a confession of faith is a summary of doctrines logically ordered that are confessed by an individual church or group of churches. In other words, it is a statement of what a group believes the Bible teaches on various topics in a concise, orderly, and comprehensive manner. A catechism is a series of questions and answers written for teaching and memorization. A Christian catechism aims to teach people Christian truth or doctrines in a memorable manner. Both confessions and catechisms have been used for great profit by Christians throughout church history.

Why?

Now that confessions and catechisms have been defined, it is time to consider why you or your church might use them for discipleship. Below are four of what could be many more reasons.

They were written for discipleship

Even if confessions and catechisms weren't intended by their original framers for discipleship, we still might find them of use. However, the framers themselves wrote them for this very purpose. Consider the two documents used in my curriculum as examples below.

First, the framers of 2LBCF say their rationale for publishing the confession and include that it is for the spiritual formation of those who read it.

Confessing Sound Words

One thing that greatly prevailed with us to undertake this work was (not only to give a full account of ourselves to those Christians that differ from us about the subject of baptism, but also) the profit that might from thence arise unto those that have any account of our labours, in their instruction and establishment in the great truths of the gospel; in the clear understanding and steady belief of which our comfortable walking with God, and fruitfulness before him in all our ways is most nearly concerned.[1]

Second, both of the general assemblies of the Baptists in London and Bristol of 1693 mention the catechism that would eventually be published. The fourth resolution in the minutes of the London Assembly states it was resolved "that a Catechism be drawn up, containing the substance of Christian religion, for the instruction of children and servants, and that brother William Collins be desired to draw it up."[2]

The Bristol Assembly in a letter stated their desire that the London Churches would "remember [their] agreement at [their] last assembling, and minuted in the narrative that brother Collins should draw up a catechism and that it should be printed, a thing so needful and useful that the country have been longing to have it, and are troubled at the delay of it, and earnestly desire that you will hasten the printing of it."[3] The Bristol Assembly thought the catechism would sell, covering the printing cost, and "They think [the London Assembly] cannot do anything that will be of more general use."[4]

They work for discipleship
Next, confessions and catechisms work for discipleship. This reason is straightforward but is it true? Do confessions and catechisms work for discipleship? The answer is yes. In saying yes, I do not intend to imply that confessions and catechisms are the only things necessary for Christian discipleship. I intend to say that they are immensely helpful at assisting a Christian embrace the system of doctrine as we find it in the Bible. Catechisms and confessions can do this because they are structured in an orderly way. Catechisms can be memorized with some discipline. Each provides the most explicit scripture references to support the doctrine being promoted.

---

[1] James M. Renihan, ed., *Faith and Life for Baptists: the Documents of the London Particular Baptist General Assemblies, 1689-1694* (Palmdale, CA: RBAP, 2016), 213-214.
[2] Renihan, ed., *Faith and Life for Baptists*, 134.
[3] Renihan, ed., *Faith and Life for Baptists*, 136.
[4] Renihan, ed., *Faith and Life for Baptists*, 136.

Introduction

As I have taken two gentlemen from my church through the BC, I've noticed that they were able to articulate what the catechism is saying in their own words almost immediately. In the curriculum, I provide discussion questions that promote delving deeper into the truth stated in the catechism and some implications it has. With a study Bible, Scripture cross-references, and the scripture references within the BC, they can answer these questions with accuracy. That is not to say that it is easy. They put in the work, but the results have already been positive. Moreover, both the BC and 2LBCF work well to facilitate discussion, cultivating relationships between those involved. By developing relationships and probing theological inquiry and discovery, confessions and catechisms are helpful tools that promote discipleship and growth.

They are sound
Not only do confessions and catechisms work for discipleship, but they are sound. They articulate the healthy and life-giving doctrines of the Scripture. They structure and formulate doctrines in a way that is logical and orderly. Take the order of the 2LBCF and BC as an example: first-principles (Chapters 1-6 and Questions 1-22), the covenant (Chapters 7–20 and Questions 23–92), God-centered Christian living (Chapters 21-30 and Questions 93–114), and last things (Chapters 31–32).

Suppose one goes back and reads some of the discussions and debates during the Westminster Assembly. In that case, one will see that the framers of the Westminster Standards sought to be sound and precise in their presentation and summation of the doctrines of the Bible. Their *Annotations* on Scripture provide the exegetical rationale for why they formulated the doctrines as they did. The Westminster Standards serve as one of the foundations of the 2LBCF and BC.

My reason for mentioning the debates and *Annotations* is that they show that what we find in the 2LBCF and BC, following The Westminster Standards, wasn't adopted hastily. Where the 2LBCF and BC differ from The Westminster Standards, we may consult Baptist writings of the day on those subjects. Where they are the same, we may look at the writings consulted and written by members of the Assembly or those who accepted its confessional documents. The 2LBCF and BC, following their Christian brothers who formulated The Westminster Standards and The Savoy Declaration, sought to provide a sound summary of Biblical doctrine. In my estimation, they were successful.

In stating why they affixed Scripture references to points made in the 2LBCF, the framers of the 2LBCF show that they saw the Scriptures to be the sole infallible authority in matters of faith and obedience,

> We have also taken care to affix text of Scripture, in the margin for the confirmation of each article in our confession; in which we have studiously endeavored to select such as are most clear and pertinent, for the proof of what is asserted by us: and our earnest desire is, that all into whose hands this may come, would follow that (never enough commended) example of noble Bereans, who searched the Scriptures daily, that they might find out whether the things preached to them were so or not.[5]

The intent in producing and the soundness of the 2LBCF and BC, linked with the fact that they work for discipleship, are ample reasons one should consider using them for personal and corporate discipleship. I have already found them beneficial for my walk with Jesus and the discipleship of some within the congregation I pastor. These reasons are why I have gone forward in editing and publishing this curriculum using them. You might find them useful too. Below are some of the benefits I've witnessed in using confessions and catechisms for discipleship.

What benefits?

1. Depth

Any of the confessions of faith or catechisms written in the seventeenth century have a level of depth to them that a Christian won't get from an ordinary Sunday School class or small group. Let me give you two examples: one from the 2LBCF and another from the BC.

First, consider what the 2LBCF says in chapter 19, which covers the subject of God's Law. It starts with Adam, who "God gave... a law of universal obedience written in his heart and a particular precept of not eating of the tree of the knowledge of good and evil." God required both the law written on man's heart and the particular precept to be obeyed perfectly by Adam and his descendants. The failure to obey resulted in death. The reward for obedience was life. The confession goes further in the next paragraph to explain how the same law, the law written on Adam's heart, "continued to be a perfect rule of righteousness after the fall." It was then given at Mount Sinai in the ten commandments. Not only the moral law was given at Sinai. Positive laws were also provided. These were ceremonial and judicial in nature. These positive laws were limited to the people of Israel under that covenant. The ceremonial laws, in particular, pointed to Christ and were abrogated when he established the New Covenant. The judicial laws also passed away with that nation, and "their general equity only being of moral use." The chapter later explains that the moral law is binding upon all, including believers. Paragraph six is the longest and

---

[5] Renihan, ed., *Faith and Life for Baptists*, 215.

Introduction

shows how the law applies to the believer. This theological application is rich and of great benefit for discipleship. Consider what it says:

> Although true believers be not under the law as a covenant of works, to be thereby justified or condemned, yet it is of great use to them as well as to others, in that as a rule of life, informing them of the will of God and their duty, it directs and binds them to walk accordingly; discovering also the sinful pollutions of their natures, hearts, and lives, so as examining themselves thereby, they may come to further conviction of, humiliation for, and hatred against, sin; together with a clearer sight of the need they have of Christ and the perfection of his obedience; it is likewise of use to the regenerate to restrain their corruptions, in that it forbids sin; and the threatenings of it serve to shew what even their sins deserve, and what afflictions in this life they may expect for them, although freed from the curse and unallayed rigour thereof. The promises of it likewise shew them God's approbation of obedience, and what blessings they may expect upon the performance thereof, though not as due to them by the law as a covenant of works; so as man's doing good and refraining from evil, because the law encourageth to the one and deterreth from the other, is no evidence of his being under the law and not under grace.

Paragraph 7 shows us how the explication of the law in the preceding paragraph is perfectly complementary and consistent with the grace of God in the gospel.

Second, the catechism on the same subject the law spans from question 44 through 89. It systematically goes through each of the ten commandments, defining and applying them. Take a look at its treatment of the first commandment:

> 50. Which is the first commandment?
> The first commandment is, Thou shalt have no other gods before Me (Exodus 20:3).
>
> 51. What is required in the first commandment?
> The first commandment requireth us to know and acknowledge God to be the only true God and our God (Deuteronomy 26:17; 1 Chronicles 28:9), and to worship and glorify Him accordingly (Psalm 29:2; Matthew 4:10).
>
> 52. What is forbidden in the first commandment?
> The first commandment forbiddeth the denying (Psalm 14: 1), or not worshipping and glorifying the true God (Romans 1:21), as God and our God (Psalm 81:10, 11), and the giving of that worship and glory to any other, which is due unto him alone (Romans 1:25, 26).

> 53. What are we especially taught by these words before me, in the first commandment?
> These words before me, in the first commandment teach us, that God, who seeth all things, taketh notice of and is much displeased with the sin of having any other god (Exodus 8:5, to the end).

Taking a person through the chapter on the Law of God in 2LBCF and corresponding BC questions will give them a deeper understanding of God's law and how it applies to their lives.

2. Breadth

Not only do confessions and catechisms provide depth for discipleship, but they also provide breadth. The 2LBCF contains 32 chapters, including topics like Scripture, the church, free will, the ordinances, the final judgement, and much more. The BC has 114 questions and covers much of the same material but in short, memorable questions and answers. It also gives greater depth on the ten commandments, as mentioned above, and the Lord's Prayer.

3. Humility

In addition to the depth and breadth needed for discipleship, confessions and catechisms foster humility. They require a person to reckon with the fact that Christianity didn't begin when they came to Christ. They force them to listen to people who lived in a time different than our own, yet wrestled with the same Holy Scriptures and God who inspired them. Moreover, some of the concepts it covers are challenging to the intellect and convicting to the soul. Most importantly, the fact that many confessions and catechisms, including the 2LBCF and BC, cite copious Scripture references drives the readers to humbly see if the statements within them are true. In fact, the framers of the 2LBCF encouraged people to compare all that is within it to the Holy Scriptures:

> We have also taken care to affix text of Scripture, in the margin for the confirmation of each article in our confession; in which we have studiously endeavored to select such as are most clear and pertinent, for the proof of what is asserted by us: and our earnest desire is, that all into whose hands this may come, would follow that (never enough commended) example of noble Bereans, who searched the Scriptures daily, that they might find out whether the things preached to them were so or not.[6]

---

[6] Renihan, ed., *Faith and Life for Baptists*, 215.

4. Unity
Lastly, confessions of faith and catechisms foster unity among those who subscribe and use them for discipleship. They provide a common vocabulary. They give us those principles that are most essential to Christian belief and the distinctives of our respective Christian traditions. In my case, that is the Baptist tradition of the particular variety. I have seen this firsthand at the church I pastor. The church doesn't subscribe to the 2LBCF (for now), but using it as a discipleship tool opens the door for that possibility. The men I have been taking through it find it helpful, challenging, enlightening, and biblical. It has fostered deep conversations, which in turn have brought us closer together. In this way, among others, the 2LBCF as a discipleship tool fosters unity.

How?
The work you hold is my attempt to help you use both the LBCF and BC for discipleship in your church. It contains the entirety of the 2LBCF, and its chapter divisions are the same as the confession. Therefore, the curriculum like the confession covers a wide range of subjects and should not be completed in haste. I, for example, do one part per week with the guys I am taking through it. Some may be able to go faster; others may need to go slower. Discipleship is not a sprint. It is a marathon. Take your time. Pray a lot. Chase some rabbits. Grow together in the knowledge of God and all things as they relate to him. Structure your meeting times as you please. Mine typically go as follows: prayer requests, prayer, weekly recap, study a part from a chapter, prayer, dismiss. Sometimes we run out of time, so we pick up where we left off the following week.

All of that said, a chapter contains three to four parts: catechism, Bible study, Scripture memory, and confession. Some chapters do not have a catechism portion because no questions from the catechism pertained to the chapter of the confession.[7] Every part has discussion questions to help guide study and facilitate discussion. There is space provided to write down your answers to the questions. I encourage those I take through the curriculum to complete the portion we will discuss before the meeting. Coming to meetings prepared makes for better discussion. For the remainder of the introduction, I will suggest how one might utilize this curriculum. To do this, I will talk about each part.

---

[7] Not all BC questions are within the curriculum. I plan, however, to modernize what questions are not in the curriculum and put them on covenantconfessions.com for any who would like to use them.

Confessing Sound Words

Part 1: Catechism
For the catechism part of each chapter, I encourage memorizing both the question and the answers. Quiz and help one another recite them at the beginning of the meeting. If you opt not to memorize, then read the questions and answers before discussing the questions. Also, Scripture references are found in the footnotes.

Part 2: Bible study[8]
When you discuss the Bible study portion of a chapter, read the whole text. Go through the provided questions, accounting for the context, making observations, deducing meaning, and applying the text. Discuss whatever other questions may come up along the way. By the end of the study, one should have a good grasp of the passage and its relation to the chapter's topic.

Part 3: Scripture memory
Scripture memory is an invaluable discipline for a Christian. Thus, I provide many such verses, the context for them, and discussion questions related to them. When discussing this part, take turns reciting the memory verse(s). Help one another if someone gets stuck or forgets. There is no grade given but memorizing a passage of Scripture is reward enough.

Part 4: Confession[9]
As I wrote earlier, the entirety of the confession is within the curriculum. The final part provides the text with limited editing.[10] *Pay attention to the footnotes because I provide definitions, limited commentary on terms and concepts throughout the curriculum, or Scripture references.* You will find a corresponding super script in the Scripture proofs below showing which proofs align with each statement.

---

[8] The method utilized in this curriculum utilizes the COMA acronym, meaning Context, Observation, Meaning, and Application. This acronym and similar questions to the ones found in this curriculum can be found in David Helm's *One to One Bible Reading: A Simple Guide for Every Christian* (Sydney, NSW: Matthias Media, 2020). The above resource will also show how such a method can be practically utilized in discipling other believers. To see a similar acronym with a fuller explanation, see Jason Shane DeRouchie, *How to Understand and Apply The Old Testament: Twelve Steps from Exegesis to Theology* (Phillipsburg: P & R Publishing, 2017) and, less explicitly, see Andrew David Naselli, *How to Understand and Apply the New Testament: Twelve Steps from Exegesis to Theology* (Phillipsburg, NJ: P & R Publishing, 2017).

[9] The text of *1689 London Baptist Confession of Faith* and *Baptist Catechism* I use with the permission of the publisher, Solid Ground Christian Books. *The Baptist Confession of Faith & The Baptist Catechism* (Vestavia Hills, AL: Solid Ground Christian Books, 2014).

[10] I do not change the word order or the substance of the text. Instead, I change words like hath to has or doeth to does.

Introduction

Read each chapter of the confession slowly and maybe more than once. Underline things that are interesting or confusing. When you meet, read the chapter together, discuss the questions, and talk about anything you underlined.

A parting word

I have given you reasons to use confessions and catechisms for discipleship. I have offered suggestions on how you can use this curriculum to that end. I pray that God uses this resource to bless both you and your church by his grace and for his glory.

Preface
To the Judicious and Impartial Reader

Part 1: Catechism (Q1–2)
Q1. Who is the first and best of beings?
God is the first and best of beings.[1]
- Review the Scripture references.

- How can we demonstrate the truth that God is the first and best in our lives? What habits can we cultivate in our lives and families to show that we affirm this truth?

- What are some things we might be tempted to put before God? How might we avoid putting these things before God?

Q2. Should everyone believe there is a God?
Everyone should believe there is a God, and it is their great sin and folly who do not.[2]
- Review the Scripture references.

- What are some things in creation that remind you that there is a God?

- Are those who have no access to the Bible still guilty of sin if they do not believe in God? Why or why not?

- Why might some of the most intelligent people in the modern world reject God's existence?

Part 2: Bible Study (Isaiah 40:9–31)
Read
- Read the passage multiple times.

- Read the passage in a few different translations.

---

[1] Psalm 97:9; Isaiah 44:6; 48:12.
[2] Psalm 14:1; Hebrews 11:6.

Confessing Sound Words

- Take note of what is similar and what is different.

Context
- What sort of writing is this passage: a letter, narrative, poem, wisdom literature, and/or prophecy?

- Are there any clues about the background and the circumstance under which it was written?

- What is before and after this passage?

- Are there any persons or places that are mentioned that you do not know? (Search them out earlier in the book, or with commentary)

- Does this passage allude to or quote any Old Testament passages or events that precede this text?

- Is this passage quoted elsewhere in the Old Testament or the New Testament?

Observation
- Are there any significant sub-sections or breaks in the text?

- Who is speaking?

- What is the main point or points?

- What surprises are there? What are some things you do not understand?

- What are the keywords? What words or ideas are repeated?

Meaning
- How does this text relate to other parts of the book?

- Does this anticipate something happening in the future?

- Are there any commands?

- How does the passage relate or point to Jesus?

- What does this teach us about God?

- How could we sum up the meaning of this passage in our own words?

Application
- What are some differences between you and the original audience?

- How does this passage challenge or confirm your understanding?

- Is there some attitude you need to change?

- How does this passage call on you to change the way you live?

Part 3: Bible memory (Isaiah 44:6/Psalm 14:1)
Putting Isaiah 44:6 in context: Isaiah 44 is in the context of a promised new Exodus (40–66). Chapter 43 ends with a promise of judgement for rejecting Yahweh as Israel's only saviour. However, chapter 44 gives hope of redemption and reasserts God as the source of said salvation.
- How does having a proper view of God provide comfort for those to whom he has promised salvation?

- What are some other gods in which people place their faith?

- How might we keep ourselves from falling into the idolatry of Israel?

Putting Psalm 14:1 in context: David shows the folly of rejecting God and the hope of those who receive him.
- Why might rejecting God's existence lead to doing abominable and sinful things?

Confessing Sound Words

Part 4: Confession
Read
Purpose proposed

Courteous Reader: It is now many years[3] since divers[4] of us (with other sober Christians then living and walking in the way of the Lord that we profess) did conceive ourselves to be under a necessity of publishing a *Confession* of our faith, for the information and satisfaction of those that did not thoroughly understand what our principles were, or had entertained prejudices against our profession, by reason of the strange representation of them by some men of note who had taken very wrong measures, and accordingly led others into misapprehension of us and them. This was first put forth about the year 1643 in the name of seven congregations then gathered in London. Since which time, divers impressions thereof have been dispersed abroad, and our end proposed in good measure answered, inasmuch as many (and some of those men eminent both for piety and learning) were thereby satisfied that we were no way guilty of those heterodoxies[5] and fundamental errors which had too frequently been charged upon us, without ground or occasion given on our part.

And forasmuch as that *Confession* is not now commonly to be had, and also that many others have since embraced the same truth which is owned therein, it was judged necessary by us to join together in giving a testimony to the world of our firm adhering to those wholesome principles by the publication of this which is now in your hand. And forasmuch as our method and manner of expressing our sentiments in this does vary from the former (although the substance of this matter is the same), we shall freely impart to you the reason and occasion thereof. One thing that greatly prevailed with us to undertake this work was not only to give a full account of ourselves to those Christians that differ from us about the subject of baptism, but also the profit that might from thence arise unto those that have any account of our labors in their instruction and establishment in the great truths of the gospel, in the clear understanding and steady belief of which our comfortable walking with God, and fruitfulness before Him in all our ways, is most nearly concerned. Therefore, we did conclude it necessary to express ourselves the more fully and distinctly, and

---

[3] This letter to the to the reader and the *Second London Baptist Confession of Faith* was written in 1677. The former *London Confession* was written published in 1644, making it 33 years between the two. The original confession was published to differentiate the Particular Baptist from continental Anabaptists and the General Baptist.

[4] *Divers* meaning several or various.

[5] *Heterodoxies* meaning beliefs that differ from orthodoxy, or sound doctrine.

also to fix on such a method as might be most comprehensive of those things we designed to explain our sense and belief of.

Resources referenced

Finding no defect in this regard in that fixed on by the Assembly,[6] and after them by those of the Congregational way,[7] we did readily conclude it best to retain the same order in our present Confession. Also, when we observed that those last mentioned did in their confessions (for reasons which seemed of weight both to themselves and others) choose not only to express their mind in words concurrent with the former in sense concerning all those articles wherein they were agreed, but also for the most part without any variation of the terms, we did in like manner conclude it best to follow their example in making use of the very same words with them both in these articles (which are very many) wherein our faith and doctrine are the same with theirs. This we did the more abundantly to manifest our consent with both in all the fundamental articles of the Christian religion, as also with many others whose orthodox Confessions have been published to the world on the behalf of the Protestant in diverse nations and cities—and also to convince all that we have no itch to clog religion with new words, but do readily acquiesce in that form of sound words which has been, in consent with the Holy Scriptures, used by others before us; hereby declaring, before God, angels, and men, our hearty agreement with them in that wholesome Protestant doctrine which, with so clear evidence of Scriptures, they have asserted. Some things, indeed, are in some places added, some terms omitted, and some few changed; but these alterations are of that nature as that we need not doubt any charge or suspicion of unsoundness in the faith from any of our brethren upon the account of them.

Differences and desires declared

In those things wherein we differ from others, we have expressed ourselves with all candour and plainness, that none might entertain jealousy of aught secretly lodged in our breasts that we would not the world should be acquainted with. Yet, we hope we have also observed those rules of modesty and humility as will render our

---

[6] *Assembly* meaning the Westminster Assembly of Divines (1643). This assembly of 121 theologians was appointed by parliament to make proposals for church reform. They produced among other things the Westminster Confession of Faith (1647) and the Larger and Shorter Catechisms. They taught and practiced Presbyterian church polity and infant baptism.

[7] *Congregational Way* meaning dissenting Congregationalists who met in 1658 and drafted the *Savoy Declaration*. It is almost identical to *Westminster Confession* except in the article on church government. They taught and practiced congregational polity and infant baptism.

freedom in this respect inoffensive, even to those whose sentiments are different from ours.

We have also taken care to affix texts of Scripture at the bottom, for the confirmation of each article in our Confession, in which work we have studiously endeavored to select such as are most clear and pertinent for the proof of what is asserted by us. Our earnest desire is that all into whose hands this may come would follow that (never enough commended) example of the noble Bereans, who searched the Scriptures daily that they might find out whether the things preached to them were so or not (Act 17:11).

There is one thing more which we sincerely profess and earnestly desire credence in, viz.,[8] that contention is most remote from our design in all that we have done in this matter. We hope that the liberty of an ingenuous[9] unfolding our principles and opening our hearts unto our brethren, with the Scripture grounds of our faith and practice, will by none of them be either denied to us or taken ill from us. Our whole design is accomplished if we may have attained that justice, as to be measured in our principles and practice, and the judgement of both by others, according to what we have now published, which the Lord (Whose eyes are as a flame of fire) knows to be the doctrine which with our hearts we most firmly believe and sincerely endeavor to conform our lives to. And oh, that—other contentions being laid asleep—the only care and contention of all upon whom the name of our blessed Redeemer is called, might for the future be to walk humbly with their God in the exercise of all love and meekness toward each other; to perfect holiness in the fear of the Lord, each one endeavoring to have his conversation such as becometh the gospel. And also, suitable to his place and capacity, vigorously to promote in others the practice of true religion and undefiled in the sight of God our Father! And that, in this backsliding day, we might not spend our breath in fruitless complaints of the evils of others, but may every one begin at home, to reform in the first place our own hearts and ways, and then to quicken all that we may have influence upon to the same work: that if the will of God were so, none might deceive themselves by resting in and trusting to a form of godliness without the power of it, and inward experience of the efficacy of those truths that are professed by them.

Parental responsibility proclaimed

And verily, there is one spring and cause of the decay of religion in our day which we cannot but touch upon and earnestly urge a redress of, and that is the neglect of

---

[8] *viz.* meaning that is to say.
[9] *Ingenuous* meaning honest.

Preface

the worship of God in families by those to whom the charge and conduct of them is committed. May not the gross ignorance and instability of many, with the profaneness of others, be justly charged upon their parents and masters, who have not trained them up in the way wherein they ought to walk when they were young, but have neglected those frequent and solemn commands which the Lord has laid upon them, so to catechize and instruct them that their tender years might be seasoned with the knowledge of the truth of God as revealed in the Scriptures—and also by their own omission of prayer and other duties of religion of their families, together with the ill example of their loose conversation,[10] having inure[11] them first to a neglect and the contempt of all piety and religion. We know this will not excuse the blindness and wickedness of any, but certainly it will fall heavy upon those that have been thus the occasion thereof. They indeed die in their sins; but will not their blood be required of those under whose care they were, who yet permitted them to go on without warning—yea, led them into the paths of destruction? And will not the diligence of Christians with respect to the discharge of these duties in ages past rise up in judgement against and condemn many of those who would be esteemed such now?

Conclusion

We shall conclude with our earnest prayer that the God of all grace will pour out those measures of His Holy Spirit upon us, that the profession of truth may be accompanied with the sound belief and diligent practice of it by us, that His name may in all things be glorified through Jesus Christ our Lord. Amen.

Answer

- Why would a church compose and subscribe to a confession of faith?

- What is a confession of faith?

- Why would individual Christians subscribe and make use of a confession of faith?

- On what other *Confessions* is the *1689* based (see footnote 17 and 18)?

- Why did the writers use these confessions?

---

[10] *Conversation* meaning way of life.
[11] *Inured* meaning hardened.

Confessing Sound Words

- What is one of the reasons for spiritual decay in the day of those who wrote the Confession? How might confessions and catechisms be used in the remedy of this problem?

Chapter 1
The Holy Scriptures

Part 1: Catechism (Q3–6)

Q3. How may we know there is a God?

The light of nature in man and the works of God plainly declare there is a God. Still, His Word and Spirit only do it fully and effectually for the salvation of sinners.[1]

- Review the Scripture references.

- What does nature reveal to us about God? In what way is nature, or natural revelation, insufficient?

- What person of the Godhead applies and illuminates the Scriptures to us? How can we show our affirmation of this truth?

- Why is God's Word, or Holy Scripture, necessary?

Q4. What is God's Word?

The Holy Scriptures of the Old and New Testament are God's Word and the only certain rule of faith and obedience.[2]

- Review the Scripture references.

- What is included in the Christian canon and recognized as the Word of God?

- Why might we say the Holy Scriptures are the only certain rule of faith and obedience?

- What other rules might people try to introduce?

Q5. May all men make use of the Holy Scriptures?

---

[1] Psalm 19:1, 2, 3; Acts 17:24; Romans 1:19, 20; 1 Corinthians 2:10; 2 Timothy 3:15, 16.
[2] Ephesians 2:20; 2 Timothy 3:16.

Confessing Sound Words

All men are not only permitted but commanded and encouraged to read, hear, and understand the Holy Scriptures.[3]
- Review the Scripture references.

- What excuses do we make not to make use of the Holy Scriptures?

- How can a church and pastors aid their congregation in reading, hearing, and understanding the Holy Scriptures?

- What habits should we develop to ensure we make use of the Holy Scriptures?

Q6. What are the Holy Scriptures mainly about?
The Holy Scriptures are mainly about what man should believe concerning God and what duty God requires of man.[4]
- Review the Scripture references.

- Why is it essential that we understand that Scripture is mainly about what we should believe concerning God and our duty to Him?

- What are some things the Bible does not address in detail?

- What are the dangers of using the Bible to address what it is not mainly about?

Part 2: Bible Study (Psalm 19)
Read
- Read the passage multiple times.

- Read the passage in a few different translations.

- Take note of what is similar and what is different.

Context
- What sort of writing is this passage: a letter, narrative, poem, wisdom literature, and/or prophecy?

---

[3] John 5:38; 17:17–19; Acts 8:30; Revelation 1:3.
[4] 2 Timothy 1:13; 3:15, 16.

- Are there any clues about the circumstances under which it was written?

- What is before and after this passage?

- Are there any persons or places that are mentioned that you do not know? (Search them out earlier in the book or with a commentary)

- Does this passage allude to or quote any Old Testament passages or events that precede this text?

- Is this passage quoted elsewhere in the Old Testament or the New Testament?

Observation
- Are there any significant sub-sections or breaks in the text?

- Who is speaking?

- What is the main point or points?

- What surprises are there? What are some things you don't understand?

- What are the keywords? What words or ideas are repeated?

Meaning
- How does this text relate to other parts of the book?

- Does this anticipate something happening in the future?

- Are there any commands?

- How does the passage relate or point to Jesus?
- What does this teach us about God?

- How could we sum up the meaning of this passage in our own words?

Confessing Sound Words

Application
- What are some differences between you and the original audience?

- How does this passage challenge or confirm my understanding?

- Is there some attitude I need to change?

- How does this passage call on me to change the way I live?

Part 3: Bible Memory (2 Timothy 3:16, 17)
Putting 2 Timothy 3:16, 17 into context: 2 Timothy is the apostle Paul's final letter as he approached his execution. He wrote to encourage Timothy to boldness, endurance, and faithfulness. He encouraged him to stand firm in sound doctrine as the Holy Scriptures teach it. There is a warning of the godlessness of the last days in the preceding section. There is an encouragement to preach the Word in the section that follows.
- What is the nature of Scripture, and what is its source?

- What does it mean to say Scripture is profitable?

- What is it profitable for?

- What is teaching?

- What is reproof?

- What is correction?

- What is training in righteousness?

- What is the purpose of Scripture's inspiration and profitability?

Part 4: Confession
Read

The Holy Scriptures

1. The Holy Scripture is the only sufficient, certain, and infallible rule of all saving knowledge, faith, and obedience.[5] Although the light of nature, and the works of creation and providence do so far manifest the goodness, wisdom, and power of God, as to leave men inexcusable; yet they are not sufficient to give that knowledge of God and his will which is necessary unto salvation.[6] Therefore it pleased the Lord at sundry[7] times and in divers[8] manners to reveal himself, and to declare that his will unto his church;[9] and afterward for the better preserving and propagating of the truth, and for the more sure establishment and comfort of the church against the corruption of the flesh, and the malice of Satan, and of the world, to commit the same wholly unto writing; which makes the Holy Scriptures to be most necessary, those former ways of God's revealing his will unto his people being now ceased.[10]

2. Under the name of Holy Scripture, or the Word of God written, are now contained all the books of the Old and New Testaments, which are these:

Of the Old Testament

> Genesis, Exodus, Leviticus, Numbers, Deuteronomy, Joshua, Judges, Ruth, 1 Samuel, 2 Samuel, 1 Kings, 2 Kings, 1 Chronicles, 2 Chronicles, Ezra, Nehemiah, Esther, Job, Psalms, Proverbs, Ecclesiastes, The Song of Solomon, Isaiah, Jeremiah, Lamentations, Ezekiel, Daniel, Hosea, Joel, Amos, Obadiah, Jonah, Micah, Nahum, Habakkuk, Zephaniah, Haggai, Zechariah, Malachi.

Of the New Testament

> Matthew, Mark, Luke, John, The Acts of the Apostles, Paul's Epistle to the Romans, 1 Corinthians, 2 Corinthians, Galatians, Ephesians, Philippians, Colossians, 1 Thessalonians, 2 Thessalonians, 1 Timothy, 2 Timothy, Titus, Philemon, Hebrews, Epistle of James, 1 Peter, 2 Peter, 1 John, 2 John, 3 John, The Epistle of Jude, Revelation.

All of which are given by the inspiration of God, to be the rule of faith and life.[11]

3. The books commonly called Apocrypha,[12] not being of divine inspiration, are no part of the canon or rule of the Scripture, and, therefore, are of no authority to

---

[5] Isaiah 8:20; Luke 16:29, 31; Ephesians 2:20; 2 Timothy 3:15–17.
[6] Psalm 19:1–3; Romans 1:19–21; 2:14, 15.
[7] *Sundry* meaning various.
[8] *Divers* meaning diverse.
[9] Hebrews 1:1.
[10] Proverbs 22:19–21; Romans 15:4; 2 Peter 1:19, 20.
[11] 2 Timothy 3:16.
[12] The Apocrypha is a collection of about fourteen pre-Christian books.

the church of God, nor to be any otherwise approved or made use of than other human writings.[13]

4. The authority of the Holy Scripture, for which it ought to be believed, dependent not upon the testimony of any man or church, but wholly upon God (who is truth itself), the author thereof; therefore it is to be received because it is the Word of God.[14]

5. We may be moved and induced by the testimony of the church of God to an high and reverent esteem of the Holy Scriptures; and the heavenliness of the matter, the efficacy of the doctrine, and the majesty of the style, the consent of all the parts, the scope of the whole (which is to give all glory to God), the full discovery it makes of the only way of man's salvation, and many other incomparable excellencies, and entire perfections thereof, are arguments whereby it does abundantly evidence itself to be the Word of God; yet notwithstanding, our full persuasion and assurance of the infallible truth, and divine authority thereof, is from the inward work of the Holy Spirit bearing witness by and with the Word in our hearts.[15]

6. The whole counsel of God concerning all things necessary for his own glory, man's salvation, faith and life, is either expressly set down or necessarily contained in the Holy Scripture: unto which nothing at any time is to be added, whether by new revelation of the Spirit, or traditions of men.[16]

Nevertheless, we acknowledge the inward illumination of the Spirit of God to be necessary for the saving understanding of such things as are revealed in the Word,[17] and that there are some circumstances concerning the worship of God, and government of the church, common to human actions and societies, which are to be ordered by the light of nature and Christian prudence, according to the general rules of the Word, which are always to be observed.[18]

7. All things in Scripture are not alike plain in themselves, nor alike clear unto all;[19] yet those things which are necessary to be known, believed and observed for salvation, are so clearly propounded[20] and opened in some place of Scripture or

---

[13] Luke 24:27, 44; Romans 3:2.
[14] 2 Thessalonians 2:13; 2 Timothy 3:16; 2 Peter 1:19-21; 1 John 5:9.
[15] John 16:13,14; 1 Corinthians 2:10-12; 1 John 2:20, 27.
[16] Galatians 1:8, 9; 2 Timothy 3:15-17.
[17] John 6:45.
[18] 1 Corinthians 2:9-12; 11:13, 14; 14:26, 40.
[19] 2 Peter 3:16.
[20] *Propounded* meaning to put forward.

other, that not only the learned, but the unlearned, in a due use of ordinary means, may attain to a sufficient understanding of them.[21]

8. The Old Testament in Hebrew (which was the native language of the people of God of old), and the New Testament in Greek (which at the time of the writing of it was most generally known to the nations),[22] being immediately inspired by God, and by his singular care and providence kept pure in all ages, are therefore authentic; so as in all controversies of religion, the church is finally to appeal to them.[23] But because these original tongues are not known to all the people of God, who have a right unto, and interest in the Scriptures, and are commanded in the fear of God to read,[24] and search them,[25] therefore they are to be translated into the vulgar language of every nation unto which they come,[26] that the Word of God dwelling plentifully in all, they may worship him in an acceptable manner, and through patience and comfort of the Scriptures may have hope.[27]

9. The infallible rule of interpretation of Scripture is the Scripture itself; and therefore when there is a question about the true and full sense of any Scripture (which is not manifold, but one), it must be searched by other places that speak more clearly.[28]

10. The supreme judge, by which all controversies of religion are to be determined, and all decrees of councils, opinions of ancient writers, doctrines of men, and private spirits, are to be examined, and in whose sentence we are to rest, can be no other but the Holy Scripture delivered by the Spirit, into which Scripture so delivered, our faith is finally resolved.[29]

Answer

- What does it mean to say Scripture is sufficient? What is Scripture sufficient for?

- What are the types of revelation? Why is Scripture necessary?

- What books are within the Holy Scriptures? What books are not?

---

[21] Psalm 19:7; Psalm 119:130.
[22] Romans 3:2.
[23] Isaiah 8:20.
[24] Acts 15:15.
[25] John 5:39.
[26] 1 Corinthians 14:6, 9, 11, 12, 24, 28.
[27] Colossians 3:16.
[28] Acts 15:15, 16; 2 Peter 1:20, 21.
[29] Matthew 22:29, 31, 32; Acts 28:23; Ephesians 2:20.

- What does it mean to say that the Scriptures are inspired?

- What are some traits required for a book to be canonical? How does a person come to full persuasion and assurances of the divinity and authority of the Scriptures?

- What is contained within the Scriptures? What is necessary for a saving understanding of them?

- What does it mean to say that Scripture is clear? Are all things equally clear within the Scriptures?

- What are the original languages of the Scriptures?

- What is the infallible rule of interpreting Scripture?

- What does it mean to say that Scripture is authoritative?

- How does the biblical portrayal of the doctrine of the Scripture in the first chapter of the Confession challenge you and encourage you?

- How will you apply what you have learned or been reminded of?

Chapter 2
Of God and of the Holy Trinity

Part 1: Catechism (Q7–9)

Q7. What is God?

God is a Spirit, infinite, eternal, and unchangeable in his being, wisdom, power, holiness, justice, goodness, and truth.[1]

- Review the Scripture references.

- What does each of the above-listed attributes mean (Spirit, infinite, eternal, unchangeable, wisdom, power, holiness, justice, goodness, and truth)?

- What is the appropriate response to God and his attributes?

- How are the above attributes comforting to those who are in a relationship with this God?

Q8. Are there many gods?

There is only one, the living and true God.[2]

- Review the Scripture references.

- What are some of the false gods discussed in the Scriptures?

- How does God assert His supremacy over them?

- What does it mean to say God is living? Why is it so important to understand that the one true God is living?

Q9. How many persons are there in the Godhead?

There are three persons in the Godhead, the Father, the Son, and the Holy Spirit. These three are one God, the same in essence, equal in power and glory.[3]

- Review the Scripture references.

---

[1] Exodus 3:14; 34:6; Job 11:7, 8, 9; Psalm 110:2; 147:5; John 4:24; James 1:17; Revelation 4:8; 15:4.
[2] Deuteronomy 6:4; Jeremiah 10:10.
[3] Matthew 28:19; 2 Corinthians 13:14.

Confessing Sound Words

- How should the truth that God is triune affect our private and corporate worship?

- Does this combat the idea that God was alone before creation and therefore created man? If so, how?

Part 2: Bible Study (Matthew 3:13–17)
Read
- Read the passage multiple times.

- Read the passage a few different translations.

- Take note of what is similar and what is different.

Context
- What sort of writing is this passage: a letter, narrative, poem, wisdom literature, and/or prophecy?

- What has happened so far? What notable characters have been introduced, and what significant events have taken place?

- What is before and after this passage?

- Are there any persons or places that are mentioned that you don't know? (Search them out earlier in the book or with a commentary)

Observation
- Who are the main characters? What do you learn about them?

- Is there any dialogue or speaking? Who speaks? What do they say?

- What is the main point or points?

- What surprises are there? What are some things you don't understand?

- What are the keywords? What words or ideas are repeated?

Meaning
- Does the author provide any commentary for the event? How does this help us understand the story?

- Is any behaviour commended or portrayed as positive? Is any behaviour rebuked or negatively portrayed?

- What does this passage teach us about Jesus (His Person and Work)?

- What does this teach us about God?

- How could we sum up the meaning of this passage in our own words?

Application
- What are some differences between you and the original audience?

- How does this passage challenge or confirm my understanding?

- Is there some attitude you need to change?

- What does this passage teach about being one of Jesus' disciples?

- How is the Trinity revealed in the present passage? What other passages help us develop the doctrine of the Trinity in more detail?

Part 3: Bible Memory (Deuteronomy 6:4; 2 Corinthians 13:14)

Putting Deuteronomy 6:4 into context: Deuteronomy is the concluding book of the Pentateuch/Torah. It contains three addresses to the generation that would enter and take the land of Canaan. It includes a retelling of what had happened in the prior generation, a retelling of the Ten Commandments, instructions for life in the land, promises of blessing for obedience, and warnings of curses for disobedience. The prior generation with Moses would not enter the promised land due to their sin.

Confessing Sound Words

This book is Moses' final words to his people. Deuteronomy 6:4 is a fundamental confessional truth that Israel is to believe and pass down.

- What commands are there in Deuteronomy 6:1-9?

- Why is it so important that Moses emphasized that there is only one God? Why is it essential for today?

- What can we do to remind ourselves of this truth and pass it to those in our sphere of influence? (spouse, kids, friends, church, co-workers?)

Putting 2 Corinthians 13:14 into context: The memory verse is the final verse in Paul's last letter to the Corinthians. In the first letter, Paul called the Corinthian church to unity within. The second one called them to unity with him. 2 Corinthians 13:14 is a short but powerful prayer for the church Paul loved and one of the most explicit trinitarian passages.

- What blessing is attributed to each member of the Trinity in the prayer? What does this blessing teach about their role in our redemption?

- How can we cultivate an awareness of God being Trinity in our life and prayer?

Part 4: Confession
Read
    1. The Lord our God is but one only living and true God;[4] whose subsistence[5] is in and of himself,[6] infinite in being and perfection; whose essence cannot be comprehended by any but himself;[7] a most pure spirit,[8] invisible, without body, parts, [9]

---

[4] Deuteronomy 6:4; 1 Corinthians 8:4, 6.
[5] *Subsistence* meaning a particular being, in this instance the confession is saying God is self-existent.
[6] Isaiah 48:12; Jeremiah 10:10.
[7] Exodus 3:14.
[8] John 4:24.
[9] *Without parts* meaning God is a simple and uncompounded being. God is his attributes.

or passions,[10] who only has immortality, dwelling in the light which no man can approach unto;[11] who is immutable,[12] immense,[13] eternal,[14] incomprehensible, almighty,[15] every way infinite, most holy,[16] most wise, most free, most absolute; working all things according to the counsel of his own immutable and most righteous will,[17] for his own glory;[18] most loving, gracious, merciful, long-suffering, abundant in goodness and truth, forgiving iniquity, transgression, and sin; the rewarder of them that diligently seek him,[19] and withal[20] most just and terrible in his judgements,[21] hating all sin,[22] and who will by no means clear the guilty.[23]

2. God, having all life,[24] glory,[25] goodness,[26] blessedness, in and of himself, is alone in and unto himself all-sufficient, not standing in need of any creature which he has made, nor deriving any glory from them,[27] but only manifesting his own glory in, by, unto, and upon them; he is the alone fountain of all being, of whom, through whom, and to whom are all things,[28] and he has most sovereign dominion over all creatures, to do by them, for them, or upon them, whatsoever himself pleases;[29] in his sight all things are open and manifest,[30] his knowledge is infinite, infallible, and independent upon the creature, so as nothing is to him contingent[31] or uncertain;[32] he is most holy in all his counsels, in all his works,[33] and in all his commands; to him

---

[10] *Without passions* meaning God is impassible. He experiences no emotional change. He does not suffer in his being.
[11] Deuteronomy 4:15, 16; 1 Timothy 1:17.
[12] Malachi 3:6.
[13] 1 Kings 8:27; Jeremiah 23:23.
[14] Psalm 90:2.
[15] Genesis 17:1.
[16] Isaiah 6:3.
[17] Psalm 115:3; Isaiah 46:10.
[18] Proverbs 16:4; Romans 11:36.
[19] Exodus 34:6, 7; Hebrews 11:6.
[20] *Withal* meaning along with, or likewise.
[21] Nehemiah 9:32, 33.
[22] Psalm 5:5, 6.
[23] Exodus 34:7; Nahum 1:2, 3
[24] John 5:26.
[25] Psalm 148:13.
[26] Psalm 119:68.
[27] Job 22:2, 3.
[28] Romans 11:34–36.
[29] Daniel 4:25, 34, 35.
[30] Hebrews 4:13.
[31] *Contingent* meaning dependent.
[32] Ezekiel 11:5; Acts 15:18.
[33] Psalm 145:17.

is due from angels and men, whatsoever worship,[34] service, or obedience, as creatures they owe unto the Creator, and whatever he is further pleased to require of them.[35]

3. In this divine and infinite Being there are three subsistences,[36] the Father, the Word (or Son), and Holy Spirit,[37] of one substance, power, and eternity, each having the whole divine essence, yet the essence undivided:[38] the Father is of none, neither begotten nor proceeding; the Son is eternally begotten of the Father;[39] the Holy Spirit proceeding from the Father and the Son;[40] all infinite, without beginning, therefore but one God, who is not to be divided in nature and being, but distinguished by several peculiar relative properties and personal relations;[41] which doctrine of the Trinity is the foundation of all our communion with God, and comfortable dependence on him

Answer

- List the attributes in the first paragraph and provide a brief definition of them.

- What responses should these attributes elicit?

- Are there any of the attributes you do not understand? If so, which ones?

- How is God related to his creatures? (See paragraph 2)

- Why might this biblical portrayal of God, his attributes and relation to his creatures be offensive/repulsive to some? Is it offensive/repulsive to you?

---

[34] Revelation 5:12-14.

[35] The last two sentences of paragraph two allude to the distinction between natural (moral) law and positive law. Moral law is eternal, written on man's heart by virtue of his creation in God's image, is summarized in the Ten Commandments, and is right because it is an extension of God's nature. Positive law is temporary and attached to specific covenantal arrangements. Positive law is right because God says so. An example of positive law was for Adam to abstain from eating of the tree of the knowledge of good and evil.

[36] *Subsistences* meaning an individual instance of a given essence. In this case, the divine essence subsist undivided and equally in the Father, Son, and Holy Spirit. Moreover, it is a different and more technical way of saying persons.

[37] Matthew 28:19; 2 Corinthians 13:14; 1 John 5:7.

[38] Exodus 3:14; John 14:11; 1 Corinthians 8:6.

[39] John 1:14, 18.

[40] John 15:26; Galatians 4:6.

[41] *Peculiar relative properties and personal relations*, meaning how they relate to and are distinguished from one another, which are referred to earlier in the paragraph. The Father is unbegotten nor preceding. The Son is eternally begotten of the Father. The Spirit proceeds from the Father and the Son.

- On the flip side of the above question, why is this biblical portrayal of God comforting?

- Look up the Nicene/Constantinople creed. How does the summary of the doctrine of the Trinity in the *Confession* compare? What might this say about the views of the framers of the *Confession* regarding the early creeds?

- Summarize the doctrine of the Trinity in your own words. What must be affirmed?

- What do you think "the Trinity is the foundation of all our communion with God, and comfortable dependence on him" means? According to this phrase, why is the doctrine or reality of the Trinity important for the Christian life and spirituality?

Chapter 3
Of God's Decree

Part 1: Catechism (Q10–11)

Q10. What are the decrees of God?

The decrees of God are his eternal purpose by which He has foreordained whatever happens according to the counsel of His will for His Glory.[1]

- Survey the Scripture references.

- When you read or hear the term decree, what comes to mind?

- What has God decreed? Is there anything that has happened that God did not decree?

- What is the basis of God's decrees?

- What is God's end in his decrees?

- Why might someone find the above answer problematic? Does this make God participate in sin? If not, then how do we address this apparent problem?

Q11. How does God execute His decrees?

God executes his decrees in the works of creation and providence.

- What is the relationship between God's works of creation and providence with His decrees? Which are logically prior?

Part 2: Bible Study (Ephesians 1:3–14)

Read

- Read the passage multiple times.

- Read the passage in a few different translations.

- Take note of what is similar and what is different.

---

[1] Isaiah 46:10; Lamentations 3:37; Romans 9:22, 23; Ephesians 1:4, 11.

Confessing Sound Words

Context
- What sort of writing is this passage: a letter, narrative, poem, wisdom literature, and/or prophecy?

- Who wrote this book? How do you know?

- Who was he writing the letter to? What can you learn about them and the situation of the letter?

- What comes immediately before this passage? Are there any clues to the connection between the text under consideration and that which comes before it?

- What comes immediately after this passage? Are there any clues to the connection between the text under consideration and that which comes after it?

Observation
- Are there any significant divisions or subpoints within the text?

- Are there any connecting words that help us trace the argument? (for, but, therefore, because)

- What is the main point or points?

- What surprises are there? What are some things you don't understand?

- What are the keywords? What words or ideas are repeated?

Meaning
- How does this passage relate to other parts later in the book? Maybe consider Ephesians 2:1–10 as a starting point.

- Does this passage say anything about Jesus? If so, what?
- What does this teach us about God?

- What does this passage say about us and our salvation?

- How could we sum up the meaning of this passage in our own words?

Application
- What are some differences between you and the original audience?

- How does this passage challenge or confirm your understanding?

- Does this passage and the truth within it call for a particular attitude or posture? If so, what? Is there some attitude you need to change?

- How does this passage call on you to live?

- What does this passage teach us about God's decree?

Part 3: Scripture Memory (Lamentations 3:37, 38)
Putting Lamentations 3:37, 38 into context: Lamentations is a collection of five poems. Each poem responds to the destruction of Jerusalem in 586 B.C. at the hands of Babylon. Chapter three is the central and longest chapter. It expresses grief while also declaring hope in God's sovereignty, goodness, and faithfulness. Our memory verses are in the middle of Chapter three and state that both calamity and good come by God's decree. He stands as sovereign over all that happens. It is in the faithful and good sovereign that the poet goes to in prayer (3:40–47), and it is in him that his confidence lies (3:48–66).
- Read all of chapter 3. How do verses 37 and 38 fit? What light do they shed on what goes before and what comes after?

- Verses 37 and 38 are questions. What is the author's anticipated answer to them? How can we know this?

- What is comforting about knowing that all, both good and bad, comes by God's sovereign decree?

- Read Genesis 50:15–21. How does this passage connect sinful human acts with God's perfectly good and just will?

- Romans 8:28 says, "And we know that for those who love God all things work together for good, for those who are called according to his purpose." How do the memory verses provide assurance that what Paul says in Romans 8:28 is true?

Part 4: Confession
Read

1. God has decreed in himself, from all eternity, by the most wise and holy counsel of his own will, freely and unchangeably, all things, whatsoever comes to pass;[2] yet so as thereby is God neither the author of sin[3] nor has fellowship with any therein;[4] nor is violence offered to the will of the creature, nor yet is the liberty or contingency of second causes[5] taken away, but rather established;[6] in which appears his wisdom in disposing all things, and power and faithfulness in accomplishing his decree.[7]

2. Although God knows whatsoever may or can come to pass, upon all supposed conditions,[8] yet has he not decreed anything, because he foresaw it as future, or as that which would come to pass upon such conditions.[9]

3. By the decree of God, for the manifestation of his glory, some men and angels are predestinated, or foreordained to eternal life through Jesus Christ,[10] to the

---

[2] Isaiah 46:10; Romans 9:15, 18; Ephesians 1:11; Hebrews 6:17.

[3] *Neither the Author of Sin.* While God does decree all things including sin, he does not sin nor tempt anyone to sin (James 1:13). He is not the immediate cause of any sin. It is the creature who immediately and willfully sins as a secondary cause. God uses sinners and their actions to accomplish his good and just purposes (Isaiah 10:5-7). They may will something for evil, but even then, God's will the same thing for good (Genesis 50:1). In other words, God permissively decrees and sovereignly rules over the sinful actions of men to God's perfect and righteous end.

[4] James 1:13; 1 John 1:5.

[5] God is the primary cause of all things. He created and sustains all things even his rational creatures. Secondary causes are the means by which God accomplishes what he wills form eternity. Some secondary causes are animate, rational, and in a sense free, namely they make decisions and act on them. When a pitcher throws a baseball, he actually throws it. God does not. The pitcher however is dependent in all his activity upon the being and power of God. God is the primary cause, while the pitcher is the secondary cause. Moreover, God did not make the pitcher throw the ball, the pitcher did this of his own will. The liberty of secondary causes is that they are free from outside coercion and not made to do anything they do not want to do. The illustration above is a slightly edited version of one given by R.C. Sproul. R. C. Sproul, *Truths We Confess: A Systematic Exposition of the Westminster Confession of Faith* (Sanford, FL: Reformation Trust Publishing, 2019), 74.

[6] John 19:11; Acts 4:27, 28.//
[7] Numbers 23:19; Ephesians 1:3-5.
[8] Acts 15:18.
[9] Romans 9:11, 13, 16, 18.
[10] Matthew 25:34; 1 Timothy 5:21.

praise of his glorious grace;[11] others being left to act in their sin to their just condemnation, to the praise of his glorious justice.[12]

4. These angels and men thus predestinated and foreordained, are particularly and unchangeably designed, and their number so certain and definite, that it cannot be either increased or diminished.[13]

5. Those of mankind that are predestinated to life, God, before the foundation of the world was laid, according to his eternal and immutable purpose, and the secret counsel and good pleasure of his will, has chosen in Christ unto everlasting glory, out of his mere free grace and love,[14] without any other thing in the creature as a condition or cause moving him thereunto.[15]

6. As God has appointed the elect unto glory, so he has, by the eternal and most free purpose of his will, foreordained all the means thereunto;[16] wherefore they who are elected, being fallen in Adam, are redeemed by Christ,[17] are effectually called unto faith in Christ, by his Spirit working in due season, are justified, adopted, sanctified,[18] and kept by his power through faith unto salvation;[19] neither are any other redeemed by Christ, or effectually called, justified, adopted, sanctified, and saved, but the elect only.[20]

7. The doctrine of the high mystery of predestination is to be handled with special prudence and care, that men attending the will of God revealed in his Word, and yielding obedience thereunto, may, from the certainty of their effectual vocation, be assured of their eternal election;[21] so shall this doctrine afford matter of praise,[22] reverence, and admiration of God, and of humility,[23] diligence, and abundant consolation to all that sincerely obey the gospel.[24]

---

[11] Ephesians 1:5, 6.
[12] Romans 9:22, 23; Jude 4.
[13] John 13:18; 2 Timothy 2:19.
[14] Romans 8:30; Ephesians 1:4, 9, 11; 1 Thessalonians 5:9; 2 Timothy 1:9.
[15] Romans 9:13, 16; Ephesians 2:5, 12.
[16] 2 Thessalonians 2:13; 1 Peter 1:2.
[17] 1 Thessalonians 5:9, 10.
[18] Romans 8:30; 2 Thessalonians 2:13.
[19] 1 Peter 1:5.
[20] John 10:26; 17:9; 6:64.
[21] 1 Thessalonians 1:4, 5; 2 Peter 1:10.
[22] Romans 11:33; Ephesians 1:6.
[23] Romans 11:5, 6, 20.
[24] Luke 10:20.

Confessing Sound Words

Answer
- What is included in God's decree? When did God make his decree?

- What is the basis of God's decree according to the Confession? What is it not based upon?

- What is the relationship between God's decree and sin?

- What is the relationship between God's decree and secondary causes?

- What is meant by the liberty of secondary causes? (see footnote)

- What does God's decree have to do with election of some to life?

- What does God's decree have to do with leaving of others in sin and the judgement of it?

- When did the predestination of some to life take place? Is this election of individuals? If so, is the number fixed?

- Why did God choose those whom he predestined to eternal life?

- Other than the end of glory for those God chose, what else did God foreordain?

- How should we handle the doctrine of predestination? How should we handle it in discussion?

- How can we make sure of our election?
- What attitude should the doctrine of predestination prompt from those who believe it?

- Why might election be a motivation for evangelism and world missions?

Chapter 4
Of Creation

Part 1: Catechism (Q12–13)

Q12. What is the work of creation?

The work of creation is God making all things by his powerful word in six days out of nothing, and all very good.[1]

- Review all the Scripture references.

- What did God make?

- What material did God use to create?

- How long did it take God to make all things?

- What was God's opinion of his creation?

- What does the doctrine of creation teach us about God? What does it teach us about his relationship with the world?

Q13. How did God create man?

God created man as male and female in his image, in knowledge, righteousness, holiness, and with dominion over the creatures.[2]

- Review all the scripture references.

- What two genders did God create man?

- Who did God make man in the image of?

- What does the Confession identify as traits of those made in God's image?

- How does the truth conveyed in the Confession motivate us to treat people with dignity, care, and respect?

---

[1] Genesis 1; Hebrews 11:3.
[2] Genesis 1:26–28; Ephesians 4:24; Colossians 3:10.

Confessing Sound Words

- How does the truth conveyed in the Confession help us to engage the current debates of gender identity?

Part 2: Bible Study (Genesis 2:4–25)

Read
- Read the passage multiple times.
- Read the passage in a few different translations.
- Take note of what is similar and what is different.

Context
- What type of literature is the passage? (Is it narrative, a gospel, prophecy, poetry, or something else?)
- What has happened so far in the story?
- What happened immediately before this passage? How do you think this passage and the one before it are connected?
- What comes immediately after this story?

Observation
- Who are the main characters in the story? What are we told about them?
- Where do the events in the story take place?
- Is there a problem in the story that needs resolution?
- What is the main point of the story or theme in the story?
- Is there anything that surprised or confused you?

Of Creation

Meaning
- Does the narrator of the story provide any commentary? If so, what does he say? How does this help give us clarity in what is being told us?

- Does anyone in the story learn something? Are they given a new command? If so, what did they learn? What were they commanded to do?

- Are there any threats made? What are they?

- Are there any promises made? What are they?

- Is this story taken up thematically, alluded to, or quoted elsewhere in the Bible? If so, what is said?

- How does this passage point to Jesus or find its ultimate fulfillment in him?

- Summarize the meaning, or big idea(s), of this passage in your own words.

Application
- What does this passage call you to believe about God?

- What does this passage call you to do? What attitude or behaviour do you need to change?

- What does this passage teach us about creation?

Part 3: Scripture Memory (Genesis 1:26, 27; Hebrews 11:3)
Putting Genesis 1:26, 27 in context: Genesis 1:26, 27 comes from the very first chapter of the very first book of the Bible. It comes after God created the world, and it is formless and void. It comes after God gives it form, creating light, sky and water, and land and vegetation. It comes after God fills it, creating stars, sun, moon, fish and birds, and animals. It is a summary and sketch of these events and does not give us every detail we might want. On the sixth day, after creating animals, we are told that God the Holy Trinity created man as the capstone of creation, made in his image, and to rule over the lower creatures.

Confessing Sound Words

- Read all of Genesis 1:1–2:3. How does what goes before and comes after the memory verses relate to them? Also, do you notice anything about the creation of man that sets it apart from how Moses describes the rest of creation?

- How does the rest of chapter 2 give us more clarity on the meaning and purpose of man's creation and what it means to be made in the image of God?

- What does it mean to be made in God's image?

- How should knowing that every person is made in God's image affect how we think of and treat people?

Putting Hebrews 11:3 in context: Hebrews 11:3 comes after an appeal to keep confidence and cleave to Christ in faith. It follows a brief definition of faith and shows what faith sees. Following the memory verse, the author gives us examples from the biblical history of those who, in faith, endured difficulty and triumphed. They triumphed because of the object of their faith, its author and perfecter, Jesus Christ (Hebrews 12:1, 2). Faith sees what the eye cannot.

- How do we know that God created the earth out of nothing?

- What does the doctrine of creation out of nothing teach us about God?

- What does it teach us about creation and its relationship to God?

- Why might believing this doctrine help us in times of difficulty?

Of Creation

Part 4: Confession

Read

1. In the beginning it pleased God the Father, Son, and Holy Spirit,[3] for the manifestation of the glory of his eternal power,[4] wisdom, and goodness, to create or make the world, and all things therein, whether visible or invisible, in the space of six days,[5] and all very good.[6]

2. After God had made all other creatures, he created man, male and female,[7] [8] with reasonable and immortal souls,[9] rendering them fit unto that life to God for which they were created; being made after the image of God, in knowledge, righteousness, and true holiness;[10] having the law of God written in their hearts,[11] and power to fulfill it, and yet under a possibility of transgressing, being left to the liberty of their own will, which was subject to change.[12]

3. Besides the law written in their hearts, they received a command not to eat of the tree of knowledge of good and evil,[13] which whilst they kept, they were happy in their communion with God, and had dominion over the creatures.[14]

Answer

- What did God create? When did God create? What does this teach us about God and creation?

---

[3] Job 26:13; John 1:2, 3; Hebrews 1:2.

[4] Romans 1:20.

[5] The confession's framers were not encumbered by the encroachment of evolutionary theory or estimates of the earth being millions or billions of years old. Thus, they had no qualms taking the narrative in Genesis at face value. Of course, this is not to say that there were no figural readings of Genesis 1 before the modern debates. That said, the confession makes its claim on the six-day literal reading. Modern attempts to reconcile the Genesis account of creation with the theories of the day are many. Some ascribe to the day-age theory, meaning that the word translated day in Genesis should be understood as indefinite periods, not literal days. Others argue that Genesis 1-11 is a type of poetic prose. I agree with the confession as the most consistent reading of the Genesis account. Three reasons lead me to this conclusion: 1) The text of Genesis 1 has all grammatical and syntactical markers of other historical narrative text. 2) The rest of Genesis (and the Bible) seems to assume the historicity of the earlier chapters. 3) The rationale behind the Sabbath command in Exodus 20:11 is the belief that God made the world in six days and rested on the seventh.

[6] Genesis 1:31; Colossians 1:16.

[7] Genesis 1:27.

[8] Modern attempts to eliminate gender distinctions are fool hardy because God has made man as male and female, a binary. The confession's framers did not hesitate in affirming both what the laws of nature and the Holy Scriptures declare. There are two genders, whatever gender one is born as, he/she remain regardless of what cosmetic changes he/she makes.

[9] Genesis 2:7.

[10] Genesis 1:26; Ecclesiastes 7:29.

[11] Genesis 3:6; Romans 2:14, 15. See also footnote 35 of chapter 2, on Moral Law.

[12] Genesis 3:6.

[13] Genesis 2:17. See also footnote 35 of chapter 2, on Positive law.

[14] Genesis 1:26, 28.

Confessing Sound Words

- Was each person in the Trinity involved in God's work of creation? If so, where do we find it in the Scriptures? List out other passages that show God the Trinity made all things.

- According to the *Confession*, how long did God take in creating everything? What are some other views? What view accounts for the teaching of the Bible? (See the footnote)

- What sets man apart from the other creatures God made?

- Was man created good and able to obey the law written on his heart and the law to not partake of the forbidden tree? Was he able to transgress these laws?

- For man to remain in his happy estate and communion with God, what was he required to do?

- How does a biblical doctrine of creation help us understand our world and the life we are to live?

Chapter 5
Of Divine Providence

Part 1: Catechism (Q14–15)

Q14. What are God's works of providence?

God's works of providence are his most holy, wise, and powerful, preserving and governing of all his creatures[1] and all their actions.[2]

- Review all the Scripture references.

- What are the limits of God's providence?

- What does it mean to say God governs and preserves?

- How should we understand this doctrine as it relates to sin and the fall?

- Why is the notion of God's providence a comfort?

Q15. What special act of providence did God exercise toward man at his creation?

When God had created man, he entered a covenant of life[3] with him on condition of perfect obedience: forbidding him to eat of the tree of the knowledge of good and evil, on pain of death.[4]

- Read all Scripture references.

- What is a covenant?

- What is the condition of the covenant of life?

- What was the consequence of disobedience?

- In what way did Adam relate to the rest of humanity? (See Rom. 5:12–21)

---

[1] *Creatures* meaning all that God created both animate and inanimate.
[2] Psalm 103:19; 104:24; 145:17; Isaiah 28:29; Matthew 10:29–31; Hebrews 1:3.
[3] *Covenant of Life* meaning the Covenant of Works made between God and Adam as the federal representative of all his offspring. The covenant blessings of life are through perfect obedience. The covenant curses of death are through any disobedience.
[4] Genesis 2:17; Galatians 3:12.

Confessing Sound Words

Part 2: Bible Study (Genesis 50:15–21)

Read
- Read the passage multiple times.
- Read the passage in a few different translations.
- Take note of what is similar and what is different.

Context
- What type of literature is the passage? (Is it narrative, a gospel, prophecy, poetry, or something else?)
- What has happened so far in the story?
- What happened immediately before this passage? How do you think this passage and the one before it are connected?
- What comes immediately after this story?

Observation
- Who are the main characters in the story? What are we told about them?
- Where do the events in the story take place?
- Is there a problem in the story that needs resolution?
- What is the main point of the story or theme in the story?
- Is there anything that surprised or confused you?

Meaning
- Does the narrator of the story provide any commentary? If so, what does he say? How does this help give us clarity in what is being told us?

Of Divine Providence

- Does anyone in the story learn something? Are they given a new command? If so, what did they learn? What were they commanded to do?

- Are there any threats made? What are they?

- Are there any promises made? What are they?

- Is this story taken up thematically, alluded to, or quoted elsewhere in the Bible? If so, what is said?

- How does this passage point to Jesus or find its ultimate fulfillment in him?

- Summarize the meaning, or big idea(s), of this passage in your own words.

Application
- What does this passage call you to believe about God?

- What does this passage call you to do? What attitude or behaviour do you need to change?

- What does this passage teach us about Divine providence?

Part 3: Scripture Memory (Psalm 103:19; Genesis 2:16, 17)

Putting Psalm 103:19 in context: Psalm 103 is beginning a fourfold series of thanksgiving Psalms that close book four of the Psalter. David begins and ends it with calls to praise (1, 2; 20–22). Verses 3–5 are praises for personal blessings received by the Psalmist. Verses 6–19 are praises for blessings received by the nation of Israel. The reason for praise given in verse 19 is God's absolute reign over all of creation.

- Read all of Psalm 103. What comes before and after verse 19? Besides God's absolute reign, what other reasons does David give to praise God?

- Where has God established His throne?

- Where does God's reign rule over?

- How does this provide security for the fulfillment of God's promises and salvation?

- What response should we have to trials and sufferings, understanding that God reigns over even these events in our lives?

Putting Genesis 2:16–17 in context: Genesis 2:4–25 zooms in on God's creation of and covenanting with man. Man is made (7). God plants a garden in Eden (8). Man is placed in the garden to work it and keep it (15). In the memory verse, we see a clue of the nature of the relationship between God and Adam. It wasn't merely natural. Man naturally was required to obey God as a creature according to the Law written on his heart. It was covenantal, meaning there was positive law (See the memory verses), or a Law that was not written on man's heart. We also see promises of blessing for obedience in the tree of life and promised curses for disobedience to the moral and positive law. The penalty of disobedience was death.

- Read Genesis 2:4–25.

- Of what trees may the man and the woman eat?

- Of what tree may the man and the woman not eat?

- What is the penalty for eating of the forbidden tree?

- How does Romans 5:12–21 help us understand the nature of Adam's relationship with God and us? How does Christ succeed where Adam failed?

- What kind of obedience is required for Adam in this covenant?

- Are there any means provided for forgiveness if this covenant is broken?

Part 4: Confession
Read
   1. God the good Creator of all things, in his infinite power and wisdom does uphold, direct, dispose, and govern all creatures and things,[5] from the greatest even

---

[5] Job 38:11; Psalm 135:6; Isaiah 46:10, 11; Hebrews 1:3.

Of Divine Providence

to the least,⁶ by his most wise and holy providence, to the end for the which they were created, according unto his infallible foreknowledge, and the free and immutable counsel of his own will; to the praise of the glory of his wisdom, power, justice, infinite goodness, and mercy.⁷

2. Although in relation to the foreknowledge and decree of God, the first cause, all things come to pass immutably and infallibly;⁸ so that there is not anything befalls⁹ any by chance, or without his providence;¹⁰ yet by the same providence he orders them to fall out according to the nature of second causes,¹¹ either necessarily, freely, or contingently.¹²

3. God, in his ordinary providence makes use of means,¹³ yet is free to work without,¹⁴ above,¹⁵ and against them¹⁶ at his pleasure.¹⁷

4. The almighty power, unsearchable wisdom, and infinite goodness of God, so far manifest themselves in his providence, that his determinate counsel extends itself even to the first fall, and all other sinful actions both of angels and men;¹⁸ and that not by a bare permission, which also he most wisely and powerfully bounds,¹⁹

---

⁶ Matthew 10:29-31.
⁷ Ephesians 1:11.
⁸ Acts 2:23.
⁹ *Befalls* meaning to happen.
¹⁰ Proverbs 16:33.
¹¹ *Secondary Causes*: See footnote 5 of chapter 3.
¹² Genesis 8:22. *Necessary* secondary causes are those means required for certain end. One example is the sun and the moon being the causes of illumination in the world (Jeremiah 31:35). *Free* secondary causes are those means a free agent might choose to get a desired end. One example is the cities of refuge a man who accidentally murdered another might freely choose to flee to for safety (Exodus 21:13; Deuteronomy 19:5). *Contingent* secondary causes are those means that's truthfulness depends upon a certain result. One example would be the legitimacy of Micaiah's status as a prophet of Yahweh was contingent or dependent upon his prophecy of King Ahab death in battle happening (1 Kings 22:28, 34). To find a more fleshed our presentation of this, see Chad Van Dixhoorn, *Confessing the Faith: A Reader's Guide to the Westminster Confession of Faith* (Edinburgh: Banner of Truth Trust, 2014), 71-72.
¹³ Isaiah 55:10, 11; Acts 27:31, 44.
¹⁴ Hosea 1:7.
¹⁵ Romans 4:19-21.
¹⁶ Daniel 3:27.
¹⁷ To accomplish his will God ordinarily uses means like rain to cause things to cause vegetation to grow and survive or the foolishness of preaching to spread his kingdom. The Scripture citations serve as good examples for how God can work without, above, or against ordinary means. Without means God promises to save Judah (Hosea 1:6). Above ordinary means God provides Sarah with a child when she is way beyond ordinary child bearing age (Romans 4:19-21). Against ordinary means God sustains Daniel's friends in the fiery furnace that consumed all that came near it (Daniel 3:27).
¹⁸ 2 Samuel 24:1, 1 Chronicles 21:1; Romans 11:32, 34.
¹⁹ *Bounds* meaning limits or confines.

and otherwise orders and governs,[20] in a manifold dispensation[21] to his most holy ends;[22] yet so, as the sinfulness of their acts proceeds only from the creatures, and not from God, who, being most holy and righteous, neither is nor can be the author or approver of sin.[23]

5. The most wise, righteous, and gracious God does oftentimes leave for a season his own children to manifold temptations and the corruptions of their own hearts, to chastise them for their former sins, or to discover unto them the hidden strength of corruption and deceitfulness of their hearts, that they may be humbled; and to raise them to a more close and constant dependence for their support upon himself; and to make them more watchful against all future occasions of sin, and for other just and holy ends.[24] So that whatsoever befalls any of his elect is by his appointment, for his glory, and their good.[25]

6. As for those wicked and ungodly men whom God, as the righteous judge, for former sin does blind and harden;[26] from them he not only withholds his grace, whereby they might have been enlightened in their understanding, and wrought upon their hearts;[27] but sometimes also withdraws the gifts which they had,[28] and exposes them to such objects as their corruption makes occasion of sin;[29] and withal, gives them over to their own lusts, the temptations of the world, and the power of Satan,[30] whereby it comes to pass that they harden themselves, under those means which God uses for the softening of others.[31]

7. As the providence of God does in general reach to all creatures, so after a more special manner it takes care of his church, and disposes of all things to the good thereof.[32]

Answer

- How does paragraph 1 describe God in its very first clause? In light of the rest of the chapter, why is it good and helpful to know that God is as the first clause describes him?

---

[20] 2 Kings 19:28; Psalm 76:10.
[21] *Dispensation* meaning an ordering, management, or administration of events.
[22] Genesis 1:20; Isaiah 10:6, 7, 12.
[23] *Author of Sin*: see footnote 3 of chapter 3; Psalm 1:21; 1 John 2:16.
[24] 2 Chronicles 32:25, 26, 31; 2 Corinthians 12:7-9.
[25] Romans 8:28.
[26] Romans 1:24, 26, 28; 11:7, 8.
[27] Deuteronomy 29:4.
[28] Matthew 13:12.
[29] Deuteronomy 2:30; 2 Kings 8:12, 13.
[30] Psalm 81:11, 12; 2 Thessalonians 2:10-12.
[31] Exodus 8:15, 32; Isaiah 6:9, 10; 1 Peter 2:7, 8.
[32] Isaiah 43:3-5; Amos 9:8, 9; 1 Timothy 4:10.

Of Divine Providence

- What is divine providence? What does God's providence cover, or what is the extent of divine providence?

- What is the relationship between divine providence and God's decree?

- What are secondary causes? What are the different kinds of secondary causes?

- What are some examples of ordinary means? Does God need to use them?

- What are some practical effects of knowing that God uses means?

- What is the relationship of God's providence to the first fall and sin?

- What are some of the reasons God might leave his own children to various temptations and the corruptions of their hearts?

- How does God blind and harden some?

- Does God show special care towards his people?

- How does confessions formulation of God's providence provide encouragement for the suffering believer? What can the believer know about the end of their suffering (Romans 8:28)?

- Consider this quote from Thomas Watson in his exposition of the Westminster Shorter Catechism, "Let us be content God should rule the world, learn to acquiesce[33] in his will and submit to his providence. Does any affliction befall you? Remember God sees it is that which is fit for you, or it should not come; your clothes cannot be so fit for you, as your crosses."[34]

---

[33] *Acquiesce* meaning to accept something.
[34] Thomas Watson, *The Select Works of the Rev. Thomas Watson, Comprising His Celebrated Body of Divinity, in a Series of Lectures on the Shorter Catechism, and Various Sermons and Treatises* (New York: Robert Carter & Brothers, 1855), 87.

Chapter 6
Of the Fall of Man, of Sin, and of the Punishment Thereof

Part 1: Catechism (Q16–22)

Q16. Did our first parents continue in the state in which they were created?
Our first parents being left to the freedom of their own will, fell from the condition in which they were created by sinning against God.[1]

- Review all Scripture references.

- What was man's created state?

- Are our first parents responsible for their fall? Why?

- How should this truth promote us to be watchful of our own sins?

Q17. What is sin?
Sin is any lack of conformity with or transgression of God's law.[2]

- Review all Scripture references.

- What are some examples of lacking conformity with God's law? Where do you fail to conform to God's law?

- What are some examples of transgressing God's law? Where do you transgress God's law?

Q18. What was the sin by which our first parents fell from the state in which they were created?
The sin by which our parents fell from the state in which they were created was their eating the forbidden fruit.[3]

- Read all Scripture references.

---

[1] Genesis 3:6–8; Ecclesiastes 7:29.
[2] 1 John 3:4.
[3] Genesis 3:6, 12.

- Was this transgression against a moral or positive law?

Q19. Did all mankind fall in Adam's first transgression?
The covenant was made with Adam as the representative for all his descendants. Thus, in his first transgression, all mankind descending from him by ordinary generation sinned in and fell with him.[4]
- Read all Scripture references.

- What is the covenant that God made with Adam?

- What type of relationship did Adam have with his descendants by ordinary generation?

- What is your initial response to know the type of relationship you have with Adam? Why might some be hostile to this notion?

Q20. Into what state did the fall bring mankind?
The fall brought mankind into a state of sin and misery.[5]
- Read all Scripture references.

Q21. Of what does the sinfulness of that state into which man fell consists?
The sinfulness of the state into which man fell consists of the guilt of Adam's first sin, the loss of original righteousness, and the corruption of his whole nature, which is commonly called original sin, together with all actual transgressions that proceed from it.[6]
- Read all Scripture references.

- Define all the things that consist in the state man fell (guilt of Adam's first sin, the loss of original righteousness, and the corruption of his whole nature).

- What is the relationship of actual sins committed by us with original sin?

---

[4] Genesis 2:16, 17; Romans 5:12; 1 Corinthians 15:21, 22.
[5] Romans 5:12.
[6] Matthew 15:19; Romans 5:12-21; Ephesians 2:1-3; James 1:14, 15.

Q22. What is the misery of that into which man fell?

All mankind by their fall lost communion with God, are under his wrath and curse, and so made liable to all miseries in this life, to death itself, and to the pains of hell forever.[7]

- Read all Scripture references.

- Define all the miseries that came from the fall (lost communion with God, under his wrath and curse, and liability to all miseries in this life, to death itself, and to the pains of hell forever.

- What miseries of life after the fall have you experienced?

Part 2: Bible Study (Romans 5:12–21)

Read

- Read the passage multiple times.

- Read the passage in a few different translations.

- Take note of what is similar and what is different.

Observation

- Are there any significant divisions or subpoints within the text?

- Are there any connecting words that help us trace the argument? (for, but, therefore, because)

- What is the main point or points?

- What surprises are there? What are some things you don't understand?

- What are the keywords? What words or ideas are repeated?

---

[7] Genesis 3:8, 10, 24; Lamentations 3:39; Matthew 25:41, 46; Romans 6:23; Galatians 3:10; Ephesians 2:2, 3.

Meaning
- How does this passage relate to other parts later in the book?

- Does this passage say anything about Jesus? If so, what?

- What does this teach us about God?

- What does this passage say about us and our salvation?

- How could we sum up the meaning of this passage in our own words?

Application
- What are some differences between you and the original audience?

- How does this passage challenge or confirm your understanding?

- Does this passage and the truth within it call for a particular attitude or posture? If so, what? Is there some attitude you need to change?

- How does this passage call on you to live?

- What does this passage teach you about the fall and sin?

Part 3: Scripture Memory (Romans 5:12; 1 John 3:4)
Putting Romans 5:12 in context: Romans is the longest letter of the apostle Paul. As such, it provides us with the most systematic presentation of the gospel, its benefits, and its effects in one book. Roman 1–11 covers the doctrines of the Gospel that must be believed, and Romans 12–16 are how we are to live in light of these doctrines. Romans 1:16-17 teaches revelation of God's righteousness in the Gospel. Romans 1:18-3:20 teaches the universal unrighteousness of humanity. Romans 3:21-5:21 teaches God's righteousness in justifying sinners in Christ by faith. Our memory verse begins a section in which Paul grounds our justification in Christ the New Adam.
- Read Romans 5:12–21.

- Where does Paul finish the comparison that he makes in verse 12?
- Who is the one man that Paul is speaking of in verse 12?

- What was his sin?

- What were the consequences of his sin?

Putting 1 John 3:4 in context: 1 John is the first of three letters written by the apostle John. In this letter, he refutes false teachers. He gives Christians different tests to check the legitimacy of our communion with God. In doing so, He drives us to 1) analyze the fruit of teachers before we listen to them and 2) to Christ as the ground and rock of our assurance. 1 John 2:28–3:10a is the test of righteousness and holy living. One who is in communion with God will seek to live in accord with His moral law. Our verse gives a definition of sin.

- Read 1 John 2:28–3:10a.

- What is the cause of us being made completely like Christ? (See 1 John 3:2)

- How is one made pure? (See 1 John 3:3)

- What does it mean to make a practice of sin?

- What is sin?

- Where do we find a summary of the law?

Part 4: Confession
Read

    1. Although God created man upright and perfect, and gave him a righteous law, which had been unto life had he kept it, and threatened death upon the breach thereof,[8] yet he did not long abide in this honour; Satan using the subtlety of the

---

[8] Genesis 2:16, 17

Confessing Sound Words

serpent to subdue Eve, then by her seducing Adam, who, without any compulsion,[9] did willfully transgress the law of their creation,[10] and the command given unto them, in eating the forbidden fruit,[11] [12] which God was pleased, according to his wise and holy counsel to permit, having purposed to order it to his own glory.

2. Our first parents, by this sin, fell from their original righteousness and communion with God, and we in them whereby death came upon all:[13] all becoming dead in sin,[14] and wholly defiled in all the faculties and parts of soul and body.[15]

3. They being the root, and by God's appointment, standing in the room and stead of all mankind, the guilt of the sin was imputed, and corrupted nature conveyed, to all their posterity descending from them by ordinary generation,[16] being now conceived in sin,[17] and by nature children of wrath,[18] the servants of sin, the subjects of death,[19] and all other miseries, spiritual, temporal, and eternal, unless the Lord Jesus set them free.[20]

4. From this original corruption, whereby we are utterly indisposed, disabled, and made opposite to all good, and wholly inclined to all evil,[21] do proceed all actual transgressions.[22]

5. The corruption of nature, during this life, does remain in those that are regenerated;[23] and although it be through Christ pardoned and mortified, yet both itself, and the first motions thereof, are truly and properly sin.[24]

Answer

- What was man's state at his creation? What did he possess? What could he earn?

- Did man stay in this state? What happened? Who was the agent that prompted this event?

---

[9] *Compulsion,* meaning force.
[10] Moral law: see footnote 35 of chapter 2.
[11] Genesis 3:12, 13; 2 Corinthians 11:3.
[12] Positive law: see footnote 35 of chapter 2.
[13] Romans 3:23.
[14] Romans 5:12.
[15] Genesis 6:5; Jeremiah 17:9; Romans 3:10–19; Titus 1:15.
[16] Romans 5:12–19; 1 Corinthians 15:21, 22, 45, 49.
[17] Job 14:4; Psalm 51:5.
[18] Ephesians 2:3.
[19] Romans 5:12; 6:20.
[20] 1 Thessalonians 1:10; Hebrews 2:14, 15.
[21] Romans 8:7; Colossians 1:21.
[22] Matthew 15:19; James 1:14, 15.
[23] Ecclesiastes 7:20; Romans 7:18,23; 1 John 1:8.
[24] Romans 7:23–25; Galatians 5:17.

Of the Fall of Man, of Sin, and of the Punishment Thereof

- The confession says of this event, "which God was pleased, according to his wise and holy counsel to permit, having purposed to order it to his own glory." What do you make of this quote?

- What does this teach us about God concerning the fall?

- What was the result of this sin? What does it have to do with us?

- What have we inherited from our first parents because of their first sin? How are these things transmitted to us?

- What is the state of the unregenerate sinner?

- What is the relationship between the regenerate and the effects of this first sin?

- How does this chapter convey the biblical teaching that we all, without exception, need a saviour and cannot save ourselves? What passages teach this?

- What virtues do the teachings of this chapter in the confession cultivate in us?

Chapter 7
Of God's Covenant

Part 1: Catechism (Q23)

Q23. Did God leave all mankind to perish in the state of sin and misery?

God, having elected some to everlasting life out of His mere good pleasure, entered into a covenant of grace to deliver them out of the state of sin and misery and to bring them into a state of salvation by a Redeemer.[1]

- Review all Scripture references.

- Did God elect all to everlasting life? If not, who did He elect? When did this take place? (see Ephesians 1:4, 5)

- What is the foundation or basis of God's election?

- What is a covenant? How does this covenant differ from the "covenant of life" in question 15?

- What does this covenant of grace accomplish for the elect?

- Who is the one that brings this about?

Part 2: Bible Study (Hebrews 8:1–13)

Read

- Read the passage multiple times.

- Read the passage in a few different translations.

- Take note of what is similar and what is different.

Context

- What sort of writing is this passage: a letter, narrative, poem, wisdom literature, and/or prophecy?

---

[1] Romans 3:20–22; Galatians 3:21, 22; Ephesians 1:4, 5.

Confessing Sound Words

- Who wrote this book? How do you know?

- Who was he writing the letter to? What can you learn about them and the situation of the letter?

- What comes immediately before this passage? Are there any clues to the connection between the text under consideration and that which comes before it?

- What comes immediately after this passage? Are there any clues to the connection between the text under consideration and that which comes after it?

Observation
- Are there any significant divisions or subpoints within the text?

- Are there any connecting words that help us trace the argument? (for, but, therefore, because)

- What is the main point or points?

- What surprises are there? What are some things you don't understand?

- What are the keywords? What words or ideas are repeated?

Meaning
- How does this passage relate to other parts later in the book?

- Does this passage say anything about Jesus? If so, what?

- What does this teach us about God?

- What does this passage say about us and our salvation?

- How could we sum up the meaning of this passage in our own words?

Application
- What are some differences between you and the original audience?

Of God's Punishments

- How does this passage challenge or confirm your understanding?

- Does this passage and the truth within it call for a particular attitude or posture? If so, what? Is there some attitude you need to change?

- How does this passage call on you to live?

- What does this passage teach us about God's Covenant of Grace/ New Covenant?

Scripture Memory (Jeremiah 31:33; Romans 8:3)

Putting Jeremiah 31:33 in context: Jeremiah prophesied for over forty years, beginning in 627/626 BC during Josiah's reign and ending sometime after the destruction of Jerusalem in 587/586 BC. His ministry spanned the rule of five kings. His book contains, among other things, warnings of coming judgement (1–25), the hope of future salvation (30–33), and oracles against the enemies of Judah (46–51). The memory verse is within the section of the hope of future salvation. The immediate context is 31:31–37, in which there is a promise of a new covenant.

- Read Jeremiah 31:31–37.

- Who is the one making this covenant?

- What covenant is it different than?

- How or why is the new covenant different? (See verses 33 and 34).

- When will this covenant cease?

Putting Romans 8:3, 4 in context: Romans is the longest letter of the apostle Paul. Romans 1:16, 17 teaches revelation of God's righteousness in the Gospel. Romans 1:18–3:20 teaches the universal unrighteousness of humanity. Romans 3:21–5:21 teaches God's righteousness in justifying sinners in Christ by faith. Romans 6–8 teaches how the grace that justifies also reigns over the lives of those it justifies in Christ. Sin has been dethroned (6) though it still persists until the life to come (7). By the Spirit, the justified, adopted children of God in Christ combat and overcome the flesh (8). The subject taken up in 8:1–4 is our freedom from the power and condemnation of sin in Christ.

- Read Romans 8:1-11.

- What has God done?

- Why couldn't the law do it?

- How did He do it?

- What was the result?

- How is the righteous requirement of the law fulfilled in us?

Part 4: Confession
Read

1. The distance between God and the creature is so great, that although reasonable creatures do owe obedience to him as their creator, yet they could never have attained the reward of life but by some voluntary condescension on God's part, which he has been pleased to express by way of covenant.[2]

2. Moreover, man having brought himself under the curse of the law by his fall,[3] it pleased the Lord to make a covenant of grace,[4][5] wherein he freely offers unto sinners life and salvation by Jesus Christ, requiring of them faith in him, that they may be saved;[6] and promising to give unto all those that are ordained unto eternal life, his Holy Spirit, to make them willing and able to believe.[7]

3. This covenant is revealed in the gospel; first of all to Adam in the promise of salvation by the seed of the woman,[8] and afterwards by farther steps, until the full

---

[2] Job 35:7, 8; Luke 17:10.
[3] *The covenant of works*, which Adam is said to break here, is a covenant made between God and Adam as the federal representative of all his offspring. The covenant blessings of life are through perfect obedience. The covenant curses of death are through any disobedience.
[4] *The covenant of grace* is a covenant between God and the elect in Christ in which the elect receive the promised blessings of salvation by faith in Christ's active and passive obedience to the covenant of redemption and not by their own perfect obedience.
[5] Genesis 2:17; Romans 3:20, 21; Galatians 3:10.
[6] Mark 16:15, 16; John 3:16; Romans 8:3.
[7] Psalm 110:3; Ezekiel 36:26, 27; John 6:44, 45.
[8] Genesis 3:15.

discovery thereof was completed in the New Testament;[9] and it is founded in that eternal covenant[10] transaction that was between the Father and the Son about the redemption of the elect;[11] and it is alone by the grace of this covenant that all the posterity of fallen Adam that ever were saved did obtain life and blessed immortality, man being now utterly incapable of acceptance with God upon those terms on which Adam stood in his state of innocency.[12]

Answer

- Compare this chapter with the corresponding chapters in the Westminster Confession and Savoy Declaration.[13] What are some of the similarities and differences?

- What does man owe to God by virtue of his being a creature?

- What must God do for man to gain the reward of life?

- What is a covenant?

- What did it please God to do, though man had fallen under the curse of the law?

- What is offered in the covenant of grace?

- What is required of man to partake of the blessings of the covenant of grace?

- How does one come to meet these requirements, or who gifts them with what is necessary?

- How has the covenant of grace been revealed?

---

[9] Hebrews 1:1.

[10] *The covenant of redemption* is a covenant between the persons of the Godhead to save a people out of sinful humanity. The Father promises to give a people to the Son. The Son fulfills a covenant of works to become man, obey the Law, and give himself as a substitute on the cross for the people promised to him. The Spirit works in and through the Son in his incarnation, life, ministry, death, and resurrection. He also is sent by the Father and the Son to apply the redemption promised by the Father and executed by the Son in calling, regenerating, gifting faith to, and preserving the elect.

[11] 2 Timothy 1:9; Titus 1:2.

[12] John 8:56; Acts 4:12; Romans 4:1, 2; Hebrews 11:6, 13.

[13] You can see them side by side here:
https://www.proginosko.com/docs/wcf_sdfo_lbcf.html#WCF7

- At what time was it fully revealed?

- What other covenant was it founded upon?

- Is there any other way besides membership in the covenant of grace that man fallen in Adam can obtain life and immortality? Why not?

- What are some practical applications of understanding the covenant of grace as described in the confession?

- What does this chapter teach us about the nature of the Bible relating to the continuity or discontinuity of the Old and New Testament?

Chapter 8
Of Christ the Mediator

Part 1: Catechism (Q24–33)

Q24. Who is the Redeemer of God's elect?

The only Redeemer of God's elect is the Lord Jesus Christ; who, being the eternal Son of God, became man and so was and continues to be God and man in two distinct natures and one person forever.[1]

- Review all Scripture references.

- What divine person became the man Jesus? What are His two natures?

- Why is Jesus the perfectly suitable to be the Redeemer of God's elect?

Q25. How did Christ, being the Son of God, become man?

Christ, the Son of God, became man by taking to Himself a true body, and a reasonable soul; being conceived by the power of the Holy Spirit in the womb of the virgin Mary, and born of her, yet without sin.[2]

- Review all Scripture references.

- Why is it important to confess that Jesus not only true God but true man with a true body and reasonable soul?

- What does it mean to say that Jesus was without sin?

Q26. What offices does Christ execute as our redeemer?

Christ as our Redeemer executes the offices of a prophet, priest, and king, both in his state of humiliation and exaltation.[3]

- Review all Scripture references.

---

[1] Luke 1:35; John 1:14; Romans 9:5; Galatians 4:4; Colossians 2:9; 1 Timothy 2:5, 6; Hebrews 7:24, 25.

[2] Matthew 26:38; Luke 1:27, 31, 34, 35, 42; Galatians 4:4; Hebrews 2:14, 16; 4:15; 7:26; 10:5.

[3] Psalm 2:6, 8–11; Isaiah 9:6, 7; Matthew 21:5; Acts 3:22; 2 Corinthians 13:3; Hebrews 5:5–7; 12:25.

Confessing Sound Words

Q27. How does Christ execute the office of a prophet?
Christ executes the office of a prophet in revealing the will of God to us by his Word and Spirit.[4]
- Review all Scripture references.

- Why do we need Jesus to be our prophet?

Q28. How does Christ execute the office of a priest?
Christ executes the office of a priest in his once offering up himself a sacrifice to satisfy divine justice and reconcile us to God, and in making continual intercession for us.[5]
- Review all Scripture references.

- Why do we need Jesus to be our priest?

- What comfort is it to know that he in his once for all sacrifice satisfied divine justice and reconciled us to God?

- What comfort is it to know that he makes continual intercession for us?

Q29. How does God execute the office of a king?
Christ executes the office of a king by subduing us to himself, ruling and defending us, and in restraining and conquering all his and our enemies.[6]
- Review all Scripture references.

- Why do we need Jesus to be our king?

---

[4] John 1:18; 15:15; 20:31; 2 Peter 1:10–12.
[5] Hebrews 9:14, 28; 2:17; 7:24, 25.
[6] Psalm 110; Isaiah 32:1, 2, 33:22; Acts 15:14–16; 1 Corinthians 15:25.

Of Christ the Mediator

Q30. What is included in Christ's humiliation?

Christ's humiliation includes his being born in a low condition, made under the law, undergoing miseries of this life, the wrath of God, the cursed death of the cross, being buried, and continuing under the power of death for a time.[7]

- Review all Scripture references.

- Why did Jesus need to undergo humiliation?

Q31. What is included in Christ's exaltation?

Christ exaltation includes his rising again from the dead on the third day, ascending up into heaven, sitting at the right hand of God the Father, and coming to judge the world at the last day.[8]

- Review all Scripture references.

- What comfort does it provide for us who trust in Christ that he experienced not only humiliation but also exaltation?

Q32. How are we made partakers of the redemption purchased by Christ?

We are made partakers of the redemption purchased by Christ by his Holy Spirit effectually applying it to us.[9]

- Review all Scripture references.

- Why do we need the redemption purchased by Christ to be applied effectually by the Holy Spirit?

Q33. How does the Holy Spirit apply the redemption purchased by Christ to us?

The Spirit applies the redemption purchased by Christ to us by working faith in us, and by that unites us to Christ in our effectual calling (Ephesians 1:13, 14; John 6:37, 39; Ephesians 2:8; Ephesians 3:17; 1 Corinthians 1:9).

- Review all Scripture references.

---

[7] Isaiah 53:2, 3; Matthew 12:40; 27:46; Luke 2:7; 22:44; Acts 2:24–27, 31; Philippians 2:8; 1 Corinthians 15:4; Galatians 4:4; Hebrews 12:2, 3.

[8] Mark 16:19; Acts 1:11; 17:31; 1 Corinthians 15:4; Ephesians 1:20;.

[9] John 1:11–13; Titus 3:5, 6.

Confessing Sound Words

- With this question, answer and all the ones that precede it, where does the salvation of sinners come from? Put differently, to who's credit are we saved?

Part 2: Bible Study (Philippians 2:5–11)
Read
- Read the passage multiple times.

- Read the passage in a few different translations.

- Take note of what is similar and what is different.

Context
- What sort of writing is this passage: a letter, narrative, poem, wisdom literature, and/or prophecy?

- Who wrote this book? How do you know?

- Who was he writing the letter to? What can you learn about them and the situation of the letter?

- What comes immediately before this passage? Are there any clues to the connection between the text under consideration and that which comes before it?

- What comes immediately after this passage? Are there any clues to the connection between the text under consideration and that which comes after it?

Observation
- Are there any significant divisions or subpoints within the text?

- Are there any connecting words that help us trace the argument? (for, but, therefore, because)

- What is the main point or points?

- What surprises are there? What are some things you don't understand?

- What are the keywords? What words or ideas are repeated?

Meaning
- How does this passage relate to other parts later in the book?
- Does this passage say anything about Jesus? If so, what?
- What does this teach us about God?
- What does this passage say about us and our salvation?
- How could we sum up the meaning of this passage in our own words?

Application
- What are some differences between you and the original audience?
- How does this passage challenge or confirm your understanding?
- Does this passage and the truth within it call for a particular attitude or posture? If so, what? Is there some attitude you need to change?
- How does this passage call on you to live?
- What does this passage teach you about Christ the mediator?

Part 3: Scripture Memory (Hebrews 7:23–25)
Putting Hebrews 7:23–25 in context: Hebrews is a theologically dense book in which the necessity of sticking with Jesus regardless of circumstances is pressed upon the reader repeatedly. The author, who many until recently thought was Paul, grounds this charge to stick with Jesus in a rich Christology (Doctrine of Christ). Jesus is first, final, faithful, and fatal. He is God the Son incarnate. He is a prophet, priest, and king, who teaches, represents, rules his people. Our memory verses primarily deal with the nature of Jesus' priesthood.
- Read Hebrews 7.

- Who is Jesus compared to in Hebrews chapter 7?

- How does Jesus' priesthood compare to the Levitical priesthood?

- How long does Jesus' priesthood last?

- How much is Jesus' priesthood able to save?

- What is the sacrifice Jesus offered?

- How are these truths comforting to sinners? How are they comforting to you?

Part 4: Confession
Read

1. It pleased God, in His eternal purpose, to choose and ordain the Lord Jesus, his only begotten Son, according to the covenant made between them both,[10] to be the mediator between God and man;[11] the prophet,[12] priest,[13] and king;[14] head and saviour of the church,[15] the heir of all things,[16] and judge of the world;[17] unto whom he did from all eternity give a people to be his seed and to be by him in time redeemed, called, justified, sanctified, and glorified.[18]

2. The Son of God, the second person in the Holy Trinity, being very and eternal God, the brightness of the Father's glory, of one substance and equal with him who made the world, who upholds and governs all things he has made, did, when the fullness of time was come, take upon him man's nature, with all the essential properties and common infirmities thereof,[19] yet without sin;[20] being conceived by the

---

[10] The covenant of redemption: see footnote 10 of chapter 7.
[11] Isaiah 42:1; 1 Peter 1:19, 20.
[12] Acts 3:22.
[13] Hebrews 5:5, 6.
[14] Psalm 2:6; Luke 1:33.
[15] Ephesians 1:22, 23.
[16] Hebrews 1:2.
[17] Acts 17:31.
[18] Isaiah 53:10; John 17:6; Romans 8:30.
[19] John 1:14; Galatians 4:4.
[20] Romans 8:3; Hebrews 2:14, 16, 17; 4:15.

Holy Spirit in the womb of the Virgin Mary, the Holy Spirit coming down upon her: and the power of the Most High overshadowing her; and so was made of a woman of the tribe of Judah, of the seed of Abraham and David according to the Scriptures;[21] so that two whole, perfect, and distinct natures were inseparably joined together in one person, without conversion,[22] composition,[23] or confusion;[24] which person is very God and very man, yet one Christ, the only mediator between God and man.[25]

3. The Lord Jesus, in his human nature thus united to the divine, in the person of the Son, was sanctified and anointed with the Holy Spirit above measure,[26] having in Him all the treasures of wisdom and knowledge;[27] in whom it pleased the Father that all fullness should dwell,[28] to the end that being holy, harmless, undefiled,[29] and full of grace and truth,[30] he might be thoroughly furnished to execute the office of mediator and surety;[31] which office he took not upon himself, but was thereunto called by his Father;[32] who also put all power and judgement in his hand, and gave him commandment to execute the same.[33]

4. This office the Lord Jesus did most willingly undertake,[34] which that he might discharge he was made under the law,[35] and did perfectly fulfill it, and underwent the punishment due to us, which we should have borne and suffered,[36] being made sin and a curse for us;[37] enduring most grievous sorrows in his soul, and most painful

---

[21] Matthew 1:22, 23; Luke 1:27, 31, 35.

[22] *Conversion*, a process of being turned into something else. Thus, the two natures of Christ remain two separate natures in His incarnation. He is true man and true God. He is not something of a in-between, or something of a different kind.

[23] *Composition*, meaning a putting together of two parts. Thus, Christ is not half divine and half human. Neither humanity or divinity can quantified. One is either human or not human. Half human is not human at all. The same can be said of divinity. The confession and those who confess it declare that Christ is again true God and true man.

[24] *Confusion*, meaning a failure to distinguish between things. Thus, it is necessary for a distinction to be made two natures of Christ.

[25] Romans 9:5; 1 Timothy 2:5.
[26] Psalm 45:7; Acts 10:38; John 3:34.
[27] Colossians 2:3.
[28] Colossians 1:19.
[29] Hebrews 7:26.
[30] John 1:14.
[31] Hebrews 7:22.
[32] Hebrews 5:5.
[33] Matthew 28:18; John 5:22, 27; Acts 2:36.
[34] Psalm 40:7, 8; John 10:18; Hebrews 10:5-10.
[35] Matthew 3:15; Galatians 4:4.
[36] Isaiah 53:6; Galatians 3:13; 1 Peter 3:18.
[37] 2 Corinthians 5:21.

sufferings in his body;[38] was crucified, and died, and remained in the state of the dead, yet saw no corruption:[39] on the third day he arose from the dead[40] with the same body in which he suffered,[41] with which he also ascended into heaven,[42] and there sits at the right hand of his Father making intercession,[43] and shall return to judge men and angels at the end of the world.[44]

5. The Lord Jesus, by his perfect obedience and sacrifice of himself,[45] which he through the eternal Spirit once offered up unto God, has fully satisfied the justice of God,[46] procured reconciliation, and purchased an everlasting inheritance in the kingdom of heaven, for all those whom the Father has given unto Him.[47]

6. Although the price of redemption was not actually paid by Christ till after his incarnation, yet the virtue, efficacy, and benefit thereof were communicated to the elect in all ages, successively from the beginning of the world, in and by those promises, types, and sacrifices wherein he was revealed, and signified to be the seed which should bruise the serpent's head;[48] and the Lamb slain from the foundation of the world,[49] being the same yesterday, and today and forever.[50]

7. Christ, in the work of mediation, acts according to both natures, by each nature doing that which is proper to itself; yet by reason of the unity of the person, that which is proper to one nature is sometimes in Scripture, attributed to the person denominated by the other nature.[51]

8. To all those for whom Christ has obtained eternal redemption, he does certainly and effectually apply and communicate the same, making intercession for them;[52] uniting them to himself by his Spirit, revealing unto them, in and by his

---

[38] Matthew 26:37, 38; 27:46; Luke 22:44.
[39] Acts 13:37.
[40] 1 Corinthians 15:3, 4.
[41] John 20:25, 27.
[42] Mark 16:19; Acts 1:9-11.
[43] Romans 8:34; Hebrews 9:24.
[44] Acts 1:11; 10:42; Romans 14:9, 10; 2 Peter 2:4.
[45] The active and passive obedience of Christ are here confessed as accomplishing the salvation of the elect. Jesus' active obedience is his obedience to the law of God in the stead of his people. His passive obedience is his willingly undergoing the punishment due his people on the cross. Put differently, What we could not do; He did for us. What we deserved; He underwent in our place.
[46] Romans 3:25, 26; Hebrews 9:14; 10:14;.
[47] John 17:2; Hebrews 9:15.
[48] 1 Corinthians 4:10; Hebrews 4:2; 1 Peter 1:10, 11.
[49] Revelation 13:8.
[50] Hebrews 13:8.
[51] John 3:13; Acts 20:28.
[52] John 6:37; 10:15, 16.

Of Christ the Mediator

Word, the mystery of salvation, persuading them to believe and obey,[53] governing their hearts by his Word and Spirit,[54] and overcoming all their enemies by his almighty power and wisdom,[55] in such manner and ways as are most consonant to his wonderful and unsearchable dispensation; and all of free and absolute grace, without any condition foreseen in them to procure it.[56]

9. This office of mediator between God and man is proper only to Christ, who is the prophet, priest, and king of the church of God; and may not be either in whole, or any part thereof, transferred from him to any other.[57]

10. This number and order of offices is necessary; for in respect of our ignorance, we stand in need of his prophetic office;[58] and in respect of our alienation from God, and imperfection of the best of our services, we need his priestly office to reconcile us and present us acceptable unto God;[59] and in respect to our averseness and utter inability to return to God, and for our rescue and security from our spiritual adversaries, we need his kingly office to convince, subdue, draw, uphold, deliver, and preserve us to his heavenly kingdom.[60]

Answer

- What is the origin or basis of God's choosing and foreordaining the Lord Jesus to be the mediator between God and man? What are the three offices of Christ as the mediator between God and man?

- Which person of the Trinity became the man Jesus? What is Jesus? How would you describe the incarnation to someone who had never heard of it?

- Who sanctified and empowered the Lord Jesus according to his human nature? What was the result of this sanctification in Jesus' life as it relates to God's law and the plan of redemption?

- What is the work of Christ? (Summarize paragraph 4)

---

[53] John 17:6, 9; Romans 5:10; Ephesians 1:9; 1 John 5:20.
[54] Romans 8:9, 14.
[55] Psalm 110:1; 1 Corinthians 15:25, 26.
[56] John 3:8; Ephesians 1:8.
[57] 1 Timothy 2:5.
[58] John 1:18.
[59] Galatians 5:17; Colossians 1:21.
[60] Psalm 110:3; Luke 1:74, 75; John 16:8.

Confessing Sound Words

- How is the active and passive obedience of Jesus related to the salvation of the elect? (See paragraph 5)

- How does the work of Christ relate to the sacrifices of the Old Testament? How are the elect of the Old Testament saved?

- Put paragraph seven in your own words.

- For whom did Jesus obtain eternal redemption? How do they come to receive the benefits of this redemption?

- Are the offices of Christ able to be transferred to any other person?

- Please list and state the necessity of each office of Christ. (See paragraph 10)

- What comforts does the Christian find in this chapter?

Chapter 9
Of Free Will

Part 1: Bible Study (Matthew 17:9–13)

Read
- Read the passage multiple times.

- Read the passage in a few different translations.

- Take note of what is similar and what is different.

Context
- What sort of writing is this passage: a letter, narrative, poem, wisdom literature, and/or prophecy?

- What has happened so far? What notable characters have been introduced, and what significant events have taken place?

- What is before and after this passage?

- Are there any persons or places that are mentioned that you don't know? (Search them out earlier in the book or with a commentary)

Observation
- Who are the main characters? What do you learn about them?

- Is there any dialogue or speaking? Who speaks? What do they say?

- What is the main point or points?

- What surprises are there? What are some things you don't understand?

- What are the keywords? What words or ideas are repeated?

Confessing Sound Words

Meaning
- Does the author provide any commentary for the event? How does this help us understand the story?

- Is any behaviour commended or portrayed as positive? Is any behaviour rebuked or negatively portrayed?

- What does this passage teach us about Jesus (His Person and Work)?

- What does this teach us about God?

- How could we sum up the meaning of this passage in our own words?

Application
- What are some differences between you and the original audience?

- How does this passage challenge or confirm my understanding?

- Is there some attitude you need to change?

- What does this passage teach about being one of Jesus' disciples?

- What does this passage teach us about the concept of free will?

Part 2: Scripture Memory (Deuteronomy 30:19; Ephesians 2:1)
Putting Deuteronomy 30:19 into context: Deuteronomy is the concluding book of the Pentateuch/Torah. It contains three addresses to the generation that would enter and take the land of Canaan. It includes a retelling of what had happened in the prior generation, a retelling of the Ten Commandments, instructions for life in the land, promises of blessing for obedience, and warnings of curses for disobedience. The prior generation with Moses would not enter the promised land due to their sin. This book is Moses' final words to His people. The memory verse provides the condition of works for Israel's reception of blessing in the land of Canaan.
- Read Deuteronomy 30:11–20.

- What does this passage teach about human choice?

Of Free Will

- What are the consequences for choosing wrongly?

- What are the promises for choosing rightly?

Putting Ephesians 2:1 into context: Ephesians is a summary of the gospel. The Triune God accomplishes salvation that the Father plans, the Son executes, and the Spirit applies (1:3-14). It prompts prayer (1:15-23; 3:13-21). This salvation manifest in the life of individuals who were dead in sin, but are now made alive in Christ by grace through faith (2:1-10). It has corporate and cosmic effects that are revealed in history (2:11-3:13). The salvation God has accomplished by grace through faith works itself out in the lives of those who experience it (4:1-5:17), affecting every relationship (5:18-6:9) and calling them to arms against the forces of darkness (6:10-20). The memory verse gives us a glimpse at sins' parasitic effects on human nature.

- Read Ephesians 2:1-10.

- What does it mean to be dead in this context?

- What are we dead in?

- What are trespasses and sins?

- Who are we said to follow?

- What end should we expect in our sinful condition?

- What must happen to change this end?

- How does this text give us some insight into human will after the Fall?

Part 3: Confession

Read

1. God has endued[1] the will of man with that natural liberty and power of acting upon choice, that it is neither forced, nor by any necessity of nature determined to do good or evil.[2]

2. Man, in his state of innocency, had freedom and power to will and to do that which was good and well-pleasing to God,[3] but yet was unstable, so that he might fall from it.[4]

3. Man, by his fall into a state of sin, has wholly lost all ability of will to any spiritual good accompanying salvation;[5] so as a natural man, being altogether averse from that good, and dead in sin,[6] is not able by his own strength to convert himself, or to prepare himself thereunto.[7]

4. When God converts a sinner, and translates him into the state of grace, he frees him from his natural bondage under sin,[8] and by his grace alone enables him freely to will and to do that which is spiritually good;[9] yet so as that by reason of his remaining corruptions, he does not perfectly, nor only will, that which is good, but does also will that which is evil.[10]

5. This will of man is made perfectly and immutably free to good alone in the state of glory only.[11]

Answer

- What does it mean for the human will to be free?

- How is human free will related to God's decree, creation, and providence? What limits do these doctrines put on the confessions presentation of free will?

- What did man's will look like in the garden?

- What is man's will like after the fall?

---

[1] *Endued,* meaning to invest with a power or quality.
[2] Deuteronomy 30:19; Matthew 17:12; James 1:14.
[3] Ecclesiastes 7:29.
[4] Genesis 3:6.
[5] Romans 5:6; 8:7.
[6] Ephesians 2:1, 5.
[7] John 6:44; Titus 3:3-5.
[8] John 8:36; Colossians 1:13.
[9] Philippians 2:13.
[10] Romans 7:15, 18, 19, 21, 23.
[11] Ephesians 4:13.

Of Free Will

- What does the regenerated man's will look like?

- What is man's will like the state of glory?

Chapter 10
Of Effectual Calling

Catechism (Q34–35)

Q34. What is effectual calling?

Effectual calling is the work of God's Spirit in which he persuades and enables us to embrace Christ freely offered to us in the gospel by convincing us of our sin and misery, enlightening our minds in the knowledge of Christ, and renewing our wills.[1]

- Review all Scripture references.

- Who is the cause or source of effectual calling?

- What is the end or result of effectual calling?

- What leads to the end or result of effectual calling?

- Why is effectual calling necessary?

Q35. What benefits do those who are effectually called receive in this life?

Those who are effectually called receive justification, adoption, sanctification, and the several benefits which either accompany or flow from them in this life.[2]

- Review all Scripture references.

- Define justification, adoption, and sanctification.

- What are some of "the several benefits which either accompany or flow from" justification, adoption, and sanctification?

- How should we respond to the reception of such benefits?

---

[1] Ezekiel 36:26, 27; John 6:44, 45; Acts 2:37; 26:18; Philippians 2:13; 2 Thessalonians 2:13, 14; 2 Timothy 1:9.

[2] Romans 8:30; 1 Corinthians 1:30; Ephesians 1:5.

Confessing Sound Words

Bible Study (2 Thessalonians 2:13–17)
Read
- Read the passage multiple times.

- Read the passage in a few different translations.

- Take note of what is similar and what is different.

Context
- What sort of writing is this passage: a letter, narrative, poem, wisdom literature, and/or prophecy?

- Who wrote this book? How do you know?

- Who was he writing the letter to? What can you learn about them and the situation of the letter?

- What comes immediately before this passage? Are there any clues to the connection between the text under consideration and that which comes before it?

- What comes immediately after this passage? Are there any clues to the connection between the text under consideration and that which comes after it?

Observation
- Are there any significant divisions or subpoints within the text?

- Are there any connecting words that help us trace the argument? (for, but, therefore, because)

- What is the main point or points?

- What surprises are there? What are some things you don't understand?

- What are the keywords? What words or ideas are repeated?

Of Effectual Calling

Meaning
- How does this passage relate to other parts later in the book?
- Does this passage say anything about Jesus? If so, what?
- What does this teach us about God?
- What does this passage say about us and our salvation?
- How could we sum up the meaning of this passage in our own words?

Application
- What are some differences between you and the original audience?
- How does this passage challenge or confirm your understanding?
- Does this passage and the truth within it call for a particular attitude or posture? If so, what? Is there some attitude you need to change?
- How does this passage call on you to live?
- What does this passage teach you about effectual calling?

Scripture Memory (John 6:44; Romans 8:30)
Putting John 6:44 into context: In John 6:22-59, Jesus teaches a crowd that he is the bread of life (John 6:35). Not long before this, Jesus is said to have fed over five thousand people with five loaves of bread and two fish (John 6:1-15). This section provides the first of seven "I am" statements (John 6:35; 8:12; 10:7-9; 10:11; 11:25; 14:6; 15:1-5). Jesus does spiritually what manna did in the wilderness physically. He gives life and sustenance. He gets people to the eternal promised land. How does one come to partake of Christ, the bread of life? This question is answered by John 6:44, 45.
- Read John 6:22-59.
- Is everyone called by the Father? How do we know?

Confessing Sound Words

- What happens to all those the Father calls?

- How does this teach that the call spoken of here is effectual/internal and not general/outward?

- How might the concept taught by Christ in John 6:44 give confidence to those who evangelize the lost?

Putting Romans 8:30 into context: Romans is the longest letter of the apostle Paul. Romans 1:16, 17 teaches revelation of God's righteousness in the Gospel. Romans 1:18–3:20 teaches the universal unrighteousness of humanity. Romans 3:21–5:21 teaches God's righteousness in justifying sinners in Christ by faith. Romans 6–8 teaches how the grace that justifies also reigns over the lives of those it justifies in Christ. Romans 8:28–30 provide comfort and assurance in the certainty of salvation for those who believe in Christ by anchoring it in the purpose of God that never fails.

- Read Romans 8:18–30.

- Romans 8:28 is a cherished verse by many (as it should be). How do the next two verses strengthen and anchor the true conveyed 8:28?

- How does the memory verse connect the divine decree (foreknowing and predestination) to the effectual call?

- What other blessings come to those who are effectually called?

- How does 8:30 imply that the call spoken of is effectual?

- Romans 8:30 is sometimes called "the golden chain" because of the richness of its truth and the unbreakable chain of blessings that are promised. What encouragements can we take from Romans 8:30?

Of Effectual Calling

Confession

Read

1. Those whom God has predestinated unto life, he is pleased in his appointed, and accepted time, effectually to call,[3] by his Word and Spirit, out of that state of sin and death in which they are by nature, to grace and salvation by Jesus Christ;[4] enlightening their minds spiritually and savingly to understand the things of God;[5] taking away their heart of stone, and giving unto them a heart of flesh;[6] renewing their wills, and by his almighty power determining them to that which is good, and effectually drawing them to Jesus Christ;[7] yet so as they come most freely, being made willing by his grace.[8]

2. This effectual call is of God's free and special grace alone, not from anything at all foreseen in man, nor from any power or agency in the creature, co-working with his special grace,[9] the creature wholly passive therein, being dead in sins and trespasses, until being quickened and renewed by the Holy Spirit;[10] he is thereby enabled to answer this call, and to embrace the grace offered and conveyed in it, and that by no less power than that which raised up Christ from the dead.[11]

3. Elect infants dying in infancy are regenerated and saved by Christ through the Spirit;[12] who works when, and where, and how he pleases;[13] so also are all elect persons, who are incapable of being outwardly called by the ministry of the Word.

4. Others not elected, although they may be called by the ministry of the Word, and may have some common operations of the Spirit,[14] yet not being effectually drawn by the Father, they neither will nor can truly come to Christ, and therefore cannot be saved:[15] much less can men that receive not the Christian religion be saved; be they never so diligent to frame their lives according to the light of nature and the law of that religion they do profess.[16]

---

[3] Romans 8:30; 11:7; Ephesians 1:10, 11; 2 Thessalonians 2:13, 14.
[4] Ephesians 2:1-6.
[5] Acts 26:18; Ephesians 1:17, 18.
[6] Ezekiel 36:26.
[7] Deuteronomy 30:6; Ezekiel 36:27; Ephesians 1:19.
[8] Psalm 110:3; Song of Solomon 1:4.
[9] Ephesians 2:8; 2 Timothy 1:9.
[10] John 5:25; 1 Corinthians 2:14; Ephesians 2:5.
[11] Ephesians 1:19, 20.
[12] John 3:3, 5, 6.
[13] John 3:8.
[14] Matthew 13:20, 21; 22:14; Hebrews 6:4, 5.
[15] John 6:44, 45, 65; 1 John 2:24, 25.
[16] John 4:22; 17:3; Acts 4:12.

Confessing Sound Words

Answer
- What is the relationship between predestination and effectual calling? How are they connected? How are they distinct?

- Who is effectually called?

- What divine person is the primary agent in effectual calling? What is the instrument of effectual calling?

- What are the results of the effectual call?

- What is the relationship between the effectual call and free will?

- Why is effectual calling necessary?

- What do you make of paragraph three?

- What does paragraph 4 say about the non-elect? Can they be saved?

- How might we distinguish the calling by the ministry of the Word from the effectual calling?

- Will those who earnestly believe and practice religions other than Christianity be saved? Why or why not?

Chapter 11
Of Justification

Part 1: Catechism (Q36)

Q36. What is justification?

Justification is an act of God's free grace where he pardons all our sins and accepts us as righteous in his sight, only for the righteousness of Christ imputed to us and received by faith alone.[1]

- Who performs the act of justification?

- What is included in the act of justification?

- What the basis of justification? By whose righteousness are we justified?

- How is justification received?

- Of what comfort is the doctrine of justification?

- Why do we need justification?

Part 2: Bible Study (Romans 3:21–31)

Read
- Read the passage multiple times.

- Read the passage in a few different translations.

- Take note of what is similar and what is different.

Context
- What sort of writing is this passage: a letter, narrative, poem, wisdom literature, and/or prophecy?

- Who wrote this book? How do you know?

---

[1] Romans 3:24, 25; 4:6–8; 5:17–19; 2 Corinthians 5:19, 21; Galatians 2:16; Philippians 3:9.

Confessing Sound Words

- Who was he writing the letter to? What can you learn about them and the situation of the letter?

- What comes immediately before this passage? Are there any clues to the connection between the text under consideration and that which comes before it?

- What comes immediately after this passage? Are there any clues to the connection between the text under consideration and that which comes after it?

Observation

- Are there any significant divisions or subpoints within the text?

- Are there any connecting words that help us trace the argument? (for, but, therefore, because)

- What is the main point or points?

- What surprises are there? What are some things you don't understand?

- What are the keywords? What words or ideas are repeated?

Meaning

- How does this passage relate to other parts later in the book?

- Does this passage say anything about Jesus? If so, what?

- What does this teach us about God?

- What does this passage say about us and our salvation?

- How could we sum up the meaning of this passage in our own words?

Of Justification

Application
- What are some differences between you and the original audience?

- How does this passage challenge or confirm your understanding?

- Does this passage and the truth within it call for a particular attitude or posture? If so, what? Is there some attitude you need to change?

- How does this passage call on you to live?

- What does this passage teach you about justification?

Part 3: Scripture Memory (Galatians 2:16)
Putting Galatians 2:16 into context: Paul wrote this letter to a group of churches located near modern-day Turkey. He has proclaimed the gospel in these churches. This letter's purpose was to call them back to the gospel and refute the errors of those who would lead these churches away from it. There is only one gospel (Galatians 1:6–9), the gospel of free grace in Christ. Paul defends his apostolic authority in chapters one and two. He defends and explains the notion that all who place faith in Jesus partake of his salvation regardless of ethnicity in chapters 3 and 4. Paul affirms he and his companions' physical Jewish decent (2:15). However, it is not their physical descent that justifies them. It is their union with Christ by faith.
- Read Galatians 2:15–21.

- Write the verse in your own words.

- What does not justify a person?

- What does justify a person?

- Who is the object of justifying faith?

- Why can't a person be justified by works of the law?

- What are the works of the law?

- What virtues should this promote in the life of the Christian?

Confessing Sound Words

Part 4: Confession

Read

1. Those whom God effectually calls, he also freely justifies,[2] not by infusing[3] righteousness into them, but by pardoning their sins, and by accounting and accepting their persons as righteous;[4] not for anything wrought in them, or done by them, but for Christ's sake alone;[5] not by imputing faith itself, the act of believing, or any other evangelical obedience to them, as their righteousness; but by imputing[6] Christ's active obedience unto the whole law, and passive obedience in his death for their whole and sole righteousness,[7] they receiving and resting on him and his righteousness by faith, which faith they have not of themselves; it is the gift of God.[8]

2. Faith thus receiving and resting on Christ and his righteousness, is the alone instrument of justification;[9] yet it is not alone in the person justified, but is ever accompanied with all other saving graces, and is no dead faith, but works by love.[10]

3. Christ, by his obedience and death, did fully discharge the debt of all those that are justified; and did, by the sacrifice of himself in the blood of his cross, undergoing in their stead the penalty due unto them, make a proper, real, and full satisfaction to God's justice in their behalf;[11] yet, in as much as he was given by the Father for them, and his obedience and satisfaction accepted in their stead, and both freely, not for anything in them,[12] their justification is only of free grace, that both the exact justice and rich grace of God might be glorified in the justification of sinners.[13]

---

[2] Romans 3:24; 8:30

[3] *Infusing*, meaning to implant or pour something in someone. In this case, it is Christ's righteousness produced and replicated in the life of the believer. In other words, this would mean that a believer is justified by God partially by Christ righteousness and partially by that righteousness manifesting in their own life. The confession rejects this notion which is believed by the Roman Catholic Church.

[4] Romans 4:5-8; Ephesians 1:7.

[5] Romans 5:17-19; 1 Corinthians 1:30, 31.

[6] *Imputing*, meaning to count or impart something to someone. In this case, it is the righteousness of Christ in his active and passive obedience that is given to the believer. Put differently justification is not a believer being made righteous but being counted righteous by a righteousness not their own, the righteousness of Christ. Christ righteousness is received by faith.

[7] Ephesians 2:8-10; Philippians 3:8, 9.

[8] John 1:12; Romans 5:17.

[9] Romans 3:28.

[10] Galatians 5:6; James 2:17, 22, 26.

[11] Isaiah 53:5, 6; Hebrews 10:14; 1 Peter 1:18, 19.

[12] Romans 8:32; 2 Corinthians 5:21.

[13] Romans 3:26; Ephesians 1:6, 7; 2:7.

Of Justification

4. God did from all eternity decree to justify all the elect,[14] and Christ did in the fullness of time die for their sins, and rise again for their justification;[15] nevertheless, they are not justified personally, until the Holy Spirit does in time due actually apply Christ unto them.[16]

5. God does continue to forgive the sins of those that are justified,[17] and although they can never fall from the state of justification,[18] yet they may, by their sins, fall under God's fatherly displeasure;[19] and in that condition they have not usually the light of his countenance restored unto them, until they humble themselves, confess their sins, beg pardon, and renew their faith and repentance.[20]

6. The justification of believers under the Old Testament was, in all these respects, one and the same with the justification of believers under the New Testament.[21]

Answer

- Who does God justify?

- How doesn't God justify them? How does he justify them?

- How is faith related to justification?

- What accompanies saving faith?

- What is the basis of our justification? Is it of God's free grace or our works?

- When was the justification of the elect decreed? When was it accomplished? When does someone personally partake of it?

- After one has been justified, can one lose it? In what way does sin affect one's relationship with God after one has been justified?

---

[14] Galatians 3:8; 1 Timothy 2:6; 1 Peter 1:2.
[15] Romans 4:25.
[16] Colossians 1:21, 22; Titus 3:4–7.
[17] Matthew 6:12; 1 John 1:7, 9.
[18] John 10:28.
[19] Psalm 89:31–33.
[20] Psalm 32:5; 51; Matthew 26:75.
[21] Romans 4:22, 24; Galatians 3:9.

Confessing Sound Words

- What must a justified Christian do when they have fallen into sin so that they may be restored to communion with God?

- How were Old Testament believers justified?

- How does the confession's articulation of justification ensure that God receives all glory in our justification?

- How does it provide comfort for the Christian? How does it comfort you?

Chapter 12
Of Adoption

Part 1: Catechism (Q37)

Q37. What is adoption?

Adoption is an act of God's free grace where we are received into the number and have a right to all privileges of the sons of God.[1]

- Read all Scripture references.

- Who does the adopting?

- What is the basis of adoption (works or grace)?

- What are the blessings that flow from adoption?

- Who are those who have been adopted?

- What are some of the privileges of the sons of God that those adopted now partake?

Part 2: Bible Study (Galatians 4:1–7)

Read

- Read the passage multiple times.

- Read the passage in a few different translations.

- Take note of what is similar and what is different.

Context

- What sort of writing is this passage: a letter, narrative, poem, wisdom literature, and/or prophecy?

- Who wrote this book? How do you know?

---

[1] John 1:12; Romans 8:14; 1 John 3:1.

Confessing Sound Words

- Who was he writing the letter to? What can you learn about them and the situation of the letter?

- What comes immediately before this passage? Are there any clues to the connection between the text under consideration and that which comes before it?

- What comes immediately after this passage? Are there any clues to the connection between the text under consideration and that which comes after it?

Observation
- Are there any significant divisions or subpoints within the text?

- Are there any connecting words that help us trace the argument? (for, but, therefore, because)

- What is the main point or points?

- What surprises are there? What are some things you don't understand?

- What are the keywords? What words or ideas are repeated?

Meaning
- How does this passage relate to other parts later in the book?

- Does this passage say anything about Jesus? If so, what?

- What does this teach us about God?

- What does this passage say about us and our salvation?

- How could we sum up the meaning of this passage in our own words?

Application
- What are some differences between you and the original audience?

Of Adoption

- How does this passage challenge or confirm your understanding?

- Does this passage and the truth within it call for a particular attitude or posture? If so, what? Is there some attitude you need to change?

- How does this passage call on you to live?

- What does this passage teach you about adoption?

Part 3: Scripture Memory (John 1:12; Romans 8:14)

Putting John 1:14 into context: John 1:1–18 is the prologue of John's Gospel. What is found in it is further explained and demonstrated throughout his narrative. From it, we learn that Jesus is God the Word incarnate, the second member of the Trinity. John 1:12,13 tells us how one is given the right to be a child of God.
- Read John 1:1–18.

- What does this whole passage teach about Jesus?

- What does the memory verse teach about the proper response to Jesus?

- What blessings come with appropriately responding to Jesus?

- By whose grace does one respond to Jesus appropriately?

Putting Romans 8:14 into context: Romans is the longest letter of the apostle Paul. Romans 1:16, 17 teaches revelation of God's righteousness in the Gospel. Romans 1:18–3:20 teaches the universal unrighteousness of humanity. Romans 3:21–5:21 teaches God's righteousness in justifying sinners in Christ by faith. Romans 6–8 teaches how the grace that justifies also reigns over the lives of those it justifies in Christ. Romans 8:14 teach us an important aspect of the Christian life.
- Read Romans 8:1–17

- What is true of all those led by the Spirit?
- What are the implications of being led by the Spirit?

- What no longer reigns in the life of the believer?

- What should we do when we struggle against sin?

Part 4: Confession

Read

1. All those that are justified, God vouchsafed,[2] in and for the sake of his only Son Jesus Christ, to make partakers of the grace of adoption,[3] by which they are taken into the number, and enjoy the liberties and privileges of the children of God,[4] have his name put upon them,[5] receive the spirit of adoption,[6] have access to the throne of grace with boldness, are enabled to cry Abba, Father,[7] are pitied,[8] protected,[9] provided for,[10] and chastened by him as by a Father,[11] yet never cast off,[12] but sealed to the day of redemption,[13] and inherit the promises as heirs of everlasting salvation.[14]

Answer

- Who does the adopting?

- Who is adopted?

- Who is the adoption in and for?

- What does adoption mean?

- What are the privileges and liberties conveyed in adoption?

---

[2] *Vouchsafed*, meaning to confer or bestow something, usually beneficial.
[3] Ephesians 1:5; Galatians 4:4, 5.
[4] John 1:12; Romans 8:17.
[5] 2 Corinthians 6:18; Revelation 3:12.
[6] Romans 8:15.
[7] Galatians 4:6; Ephesians 2:18.
[8] Psalm 103:13.
[9] Proverbs 14:26.
[10] 1 Peter 5:7.
[11] Hebrews 12:6.
[12] Isaiah 54:8, 9; Lamentations 3:31.
[13] Ephesians 4:30.
[14] Hebrews 1:14; 6:12.

Of Adoption

- What are some of the practical applications of the grace of adoption in the life of the believer?

Chapter 13
Of Sanctification

Part 1: Catechism (Q38)
Q38. What is sanctification?

Sanctification is the work of God's free grace where we are renewed in the whole man after the image of God and are enabled more and more to die unto sin and live unto righteousness.[1]

- Read all Scripture references.

- Who performs the work of sanctification?

- What is the basis of sanctification (grace or works)?

- What are the elements within sanctification?

- How might one evaluate their sanctification? How do you know you are living more unto righteousness and less unto sin?

- What are some means that God has promised to bless in our sanctification?

Part 2: Bible Study (Romans 6:1–14)
Read
- Read the passage multiple times.

- Read the passage in a few different translations.

- Take note of what is similar and what is different.

Context
- What sort of writing is this passage: a letter, narrative, poem, wisdom literature, and/or prophecy?

---

[1] Romans 6:4, 6; Ephesians 4:23, 24; 2 Thessalonians 2:13.

Confessing Sound Words

- Who wrote this book? How do you know?

- Who was he writing the letter to? What can you learn about them and the situation of the letter?

- What comes immediately before this passage? Are there any clues to the connection between the text under consideration and that which comes before it?

- What comes immediately after this passage? Are there any clues to the connection between the text under consideration and that which comes after it?

Observation
- Are there any significant divisions or subpoints within the text?

- Are there any connecting words that help us trace the argument? (for, but, therefore, because)

- What is the main point or points?

- What surprises are there? What are some things you don't understand?

- What are the keywords? What words or ideas are repeated?

Meaning
- How does this passage relate to other parts later in the book?

- Does this passage say anything about Jesus? If so, what?

- What does this teach us about God?

- What does this passage say about us and our salvation?

- How could we sum up the meaning of this passage in our own words?

Application
- What are some differences between you and the original audience?

Of Sanctification

- How does this passage challenge or confirm your understanding?

- Does this passage and the truth within it call for a particular attitude or posture? If so, what? Is there some attitude you need to change?

- How does this passage call on you to live?

- What does this passage teach you about sanctification?

Part 3: Scripture Memory (Romans 8:29; Philippians 2:12, 13)
Putting Romans 8:29 into context: Romans is the longest letter of the apostle Paul. Romans 1:16, 17 teaches revelation of God's righteousness in the Gospel. Romans 1:18–3:20 teaches the universal unrighteousness of humanity. Romans 3:21–5:21 teaches God's righteousness in justifying sinners in Christ by faith. Romans 6–8 teaches how the grace that justifies also reigns over the lives of those it justifies in Christ. Romans 8:28–30 provide comfort and assurance in the certainty of salvation for those who believe in Christ by anchoring it in the purpose of God that never fails.
- Read Romans 8:18–30.

- What did God predestine according to this verse?

- What does it mean to be conformed to the image of his Son?

Putting Philippians 2:12–13 into context: Philippians is letter containing much thanksgiving and joy. Paul is thankful for God's work in advancing the gospel and sustaining him through suffering. Moreover, Paul calls the Philippian Christians to unity in the gospel. Philippians 2:12–13 is a charge based upon the example of our Lord Jesus.
- Read Philippians 2:12–18

- What is the command in 2:12?

- What is the ground Paul gives for obeying this command in 2:13?

Confessing Sound Words

- How does our working and God's working manifest in the life of the church according to 2:14–16?

- Why can and should we confidently pursue holiness in our own lives?

Part 4: Confession
Read

1. They who are united to Christ, effectually called, and regenerated, having a new heart and a new spirit created in them through the virtue of Christ's death and resurrection, are also farther sanctified, really and personally,[2] through the same virtue, by His Word and Spirit dwelling in them;[3] the dominion of the whole body of sin is destroyed,[4] and the several lusts thereof are more and more weakened and mortified,[5] and they more and more quickened and strengthened in all saving graces,[6] to the practice of all true holiness, without which no man shall see the Lord.[7]

2. This sanctification is throughout, in the whole man,[8] yet imperfect in this life; there abides still some remnants of corruption in every part,[9] whence[10] arises a continual and irreconcilable war; the flesh lusting against the Spirit, and the Spirit against the flesh.[11]

3. In which war, although the remaining corruption for a time may much prevail,[12] yet through the continual supply of strength from the sanctifying Spirit of Christ, the regenerate part does overcome;[13] and so the saints grow in grace, perfecting holiness in the fear of God, pressing after an heavenly life, in evangelical obedience to all the commands which Christ as Head and King, in His Word has prescribed them.[14]

Answer

- Who are those that are sanctified?

---

[2] Acts 20:32; Romans 6:5, 6.
[3] John 17:17; Ephesians 3:16–19; 1 Thessalonians 5:21–23.
[4] Romans 6:14.
[5] Galatians 5:24.
[6] Colossians 1:11.
[7] 2 Corinthians 7:1; Hebrews 12:14.
[8] 1 Thessalonians 5:23.
[9] Romans 7:18, 23.
[10] *Whence*, meaning from which.
[11] Galatians 5:17; 1 Peter 2:11.
[12] Romans 7:23.
[13] Romans 6:14.
[14] 2 Corinthians 3:18; 7:1; Ephesians 4:15, 16.

Of Sanctification

- What logically proceeds the work of sanctification? What does the confession say before "are also further sanctified"?

- What is the basis of their sanctification?

- What are the means of their sanctification?

- What person of the trinity is the agent of sanctification?

- Of what does sanctification consist? What is included in sanctification?

- What is the nature of sanctification in this life?

- What remains that leads to an irreconcilable war?

- What is meant by the third paragraph? Put it in your own words.

- How does the grace of sanctification motivate us to pursue holiness?

- How does the grace of sanctification also provide encouragement for us when we stumble and backslide in our pursuit?

Chapter 14
Of Saving Faith

Part 1: Catechism (Q90-91)[1]

Q90. What does God require of us that we may escape his wrath due to us for sin?

To escape God's wrath and curse due to us for sin, God requires of us faith in Jesus Christ, repentance unto life, with diligent use of all outward means where Christ communicates to us the benefits of redemption.[2]

- Read the Scripture references.

- Why is God's wrath and curse due to us?

- What are the two requirements?

- Of what are we to make use?

Q91. What is faith in Jesus Christ?

Faith in Jesus Christ is a saving grace, where we receive and rest upon Him alone for salvation, as He is offered to us in the gospel.[3]

- Read the Scripture references.

- Put the answer into your own words.

- Is saving faith a work performed or a grace given?

- What are the aspects of saving faith?

- Who is the object of saving faith?

- What does it mean to receive Jesus for salvation?

---

[1] After question 38, the catechism and the confession diverge in terms of order. The catechism has a lengthy series of questions on the ten commandments among other things. Some of the questions from 39-89 will appear in later chapters of the curriculum.

[2] Proverbs 2:1-6; Isaiah 55:2, 3; Acts 20:21.

[3] Isaiah 26:3, 4; John 1:12; Galatians 2:16; Philippians 3:9; Hebrews 10:39.

Confessing Sound Words

- What does it mean to rest upon Jesus for salvation?

- What is the gospel?

Part 2: Bible Study (John 3:1–21)
Read
- Read the passage multiple times.

- Read the passage in a few different translations.

- Take note of what is similar and what is different.

Context
- What sort of writing is this passage: a letter, narrative, poem, wisdom literature, and/or prophecy?

- What has happened so far? What significant characters have been introduced, and what important events have taken place?

- What is before and after this passage?

- Are there any persons or places that are mentioned that you don't know? (Search them out earlier in the book or with a commentary)

Observation
- Who are the main characters? What do you learn about them?

- Is there any dialogue or speaking? Who speaks? What do they say?

- What is the main point or points?

- What surprises are there? What are some things you don't understand?

- What are the keywords? What words or ideas are repeated?

Meaning
- Does the author provide any commentary for the event? How does this help us understand the story?

- Is any behaviour commended or portrayed as positive? Is any behaviour rebuked or negatively portrayed?

- What does this passage teach us about Jesus (His Person and Work)?

- What does this teach us about God?

- How could we sum up the meaning of this passage in our own words?

Application
- What are some differences between you and the original audience?

- How does this passage challenge or confirm my understanding?

- Is there some attitude you need to change?

- What does this passage teach about being one of Jesus' disciples?

- What does this passage teach us about faith?

Part 3: Scripture Memory (Philippians 3:8–9)
Putting Philippians 3:8, 9 into context: Philippians is a letter containing much thanksgiving and joy. In Philippians 3:1-11, Paul issues a warning to the Christians in Philippi. They must watch out for the legalists that mix the law and the gospel. Instead, they should imitate him and embrace Christ by faith for salvation.
- Read Philippians 3:1-11.

- Put the memory verses in your own words.

- What does Paul count as loss?

- Why does he count these things as loss?

Confessing Sound Words

- Whose righteousness does Paul desire to have?

- How does he receive it?

- Who gives him this righteousness?

- What does this passage teach us about saving faith?

Part 4: Confession
Read

1. The grace of faith, whereby the elect are enabled to believe to the saving of their souls, is the work of the Spirit of Christ in their hearts,[4] and is ordinarily wrought by the ministry of the Word;[5] by which also, and by the administration of baptism and the Lord's Supper, prayer, and other means appointed of God, it is increased and strengthened.[6]

2. By this faith a Christian believes to be true whatsoever is revealed in the Word for the authority of God himself,[7] and also apprehends an excellency therein above all other writings and all things in the world,[8] as it bears forth the glory of God in his attributes, the excellency of Christ in his nature and offices, and the power and fullness of the Holy Spirit in his workings and operations: and so is enabled to cast his soul upon the truth thus believed;[9] and also acts differently upon that which each particular passage thereof contains; yielding obedience to the commands,[10] trembling at the threatenings,[11] and embracing the promises of God for this life and that which is to come;[12] but the principal acts of saving faith have immediate relation to Christ, accepting, receiving, and resting upon him alone for justification, sanctification, and eternal life, by virtue of the covenant of grace.[13]

---

[4] 2 Corinthians 4:13; Ephesians 2:8.
[5] Romans 10:14, 17.
[6] Luke 17:5; Acts 20:32; 1 Peter 2:2.
[7] Acts 24:14.
[8] Psalm 27:7–10; 119:72.
[9] 2 Timothy 1:12.
[10] John 14:14.
[11] Isaiah 66:2.
[12] Hebrews 11:13.
[13] John 1:12; Acts 15:11; 16:31; Galatians 2:20.

Of Saving Faith

3. This faith, although it be different in degrees, and may be weak or strong,[14] yet it is in the least degree of it different in the kind or nature of it, as is all other saving grace, from the faith and common grace of temporary believers;[15] and therefore, though it may be many times assailed and weakened, yet it gets the victory,[16] growing up in many to the attainment of a full assurance through Christ,[17] who is both the author and finisher of our faith.[18]

Answer

- Who receives the grace of saving faith?

- What person of the Trinity is the first cause of faith?

- What does this person of the Trinity use to create faith?

- What are the means ordained by God to increase and strengthen faith?

- How does saving faith respond to the Word of God?

- What are the principal acts of saving faith?

- Who is the object of saving faith?

- Does saving faith ever differ in terms of degree or strength?

- What is the difference between saving faith and the faith and common grace of temporary believers?

- What is the end of saving faith?

---

[14] Matthew 6:30; Romans 4:19, 20; Hebrews 5:13, 14.
[15] 2 Peter 1:1.
[16] Ephesians 6:16; 1 John 5:4, 5.
[17] Hebrews 6:11, 12.
[18] Colossians 2:2; Hebrews 12:2.

Chapter 15
Of Repentance Unto Life and Salvation

Part 1: Catechism (Q92)

Q92. What is repentance unto life?

Repentance unto life is a saving grace, where a sinner, out of a true sense of his sin, and apprehension of the mercy of God in Christ, does, with grief and hatred of his sin, turn from it unto God, with full purpose of and endeavour after new obedience.[1]

- Read the Scripture references.

- Put the answer in your own words.

- What must a sinner understand to have repentance unto life?

- What are the elements of repentance unto life?

- What does a sinner turn from?

- What does a sinner turn toward?

- What does it mean to have full purpose of and endeavour after new obedience?

- What was it like when you, by God's grace, experienced repentance unto life?

Part 2: Bible Study (Ezekiel 36:22–37)

Read

- Read the passage multiple times.

- Read the passage in a few different translations.

- Take note of what is similar and what is different.

---

[1] Isaiah 1:16, 17; Jeremiah 3:22; 31:18, 19; Ezekiel 36:31; Joel 2:12; Acts 2:37, 38; 11:28; 2 Corinthians 7:11.

Confessing Sound Words

Context
- What sort of writing is this passage: a letter, narrative, poem, wisdom literature, and/or prophecy?

- Are there any clues about the circumstances under which it was written?

- What is before and after this passage?

- Are there any persons or places that are mentioned that you do not know? (Search them out earlier in the book or with a commentary)

- Does this passage allude to or quote any Old Testament passages or events that precede this text?

- Is this passage quoted elsewhere in the Old Testament or the New Testament?

Observation
- Are there any significant sub-sections or breaks in the text?

- Who is speaking?

- What is the main point or points?

- What surprises are there? What are some things you do not understand?

- What are the keywords? What words or ideas are repeated?

Meaning
- How does this text relate to other parts of the book?

- Does this anticipate something happening in the future?

- Are there any commands?

- How does the passage relate or point to Jesus?

- What does this teach us about God?

- How could we sum up the meaning of this passage in our own words?

Application
- What are some differences between you and the original audience?

- How does this passage challenge or confirm my understanding?

- Is there some attitude I need to change?

- How does this passage call on me to change the way I live?

- What does this passage teach about repentance unto life?

Part 3: Scripture Memory (Acts 2:37, 38)

Putting Acts 2:37, 38 into context: Jesus had ascended and sent the Holy Spirit upon the apostles to empower them for their ministry, namely establishing the new covenant church. Our text comes at the end of Peter's first sermon and is the response of the crowd to it.

- Read Acts 2:14–41.

- Who made up the audience of Peter's sermon?

- Summarize/outline Peter's sermon.

- Look at verse 39. What is the connection of effectual call and repentance unto life?

- How might these verses assist you in an evangelistic conversation? What will you say if someone says, "What shall I do?"

Confessing Sound Words

Part 4: Confession

Read

1. Such of the elect as are converted at riper years, having sometime lived in the state of nature, and therein served divers[2] lusts and pleasures, God in their effectual calling giveth them repentance unto life.[3]

2. Whereas there is none that does good and sins not,[4] and the best of men may, through the power and deceitfulness of their corruption dwelling in them, with the prevalency of temptation, fall into great sins and provocations; God has, in the covenant of grace,[5] mercifully provided that believers so sinning and falling be renewed through repentance unto salvation.[6]

3. This saving repentance is an evangelical grace,[7] whereby a person, being by the Holy Spirit made sensible of the manifold evils of his sin, does, by faith in Christ, humble himself for it with godly sorrow, detestation of it, and self-abhorrency,[8] praying for pardon and strength of grace, with a purpose and endeavor, by supplies of the Spirit, to walk before God unto all well-pleasing in all things.[9]

4. As repentance is to be continued through the whole course of our lives, upon the account of the body of death, and the motions thereof, so it is every man's duty to repent of his particular known sins particularly.[10]

5. Such is the provision which God has made through Christ in the covenant of grace for the preservation of believers unto salvation; that although there is no sin so small but it deserves damnation,[11] yet there is no sin so great that it shall bring damnation on them that repent,[12] which makes the constant preaching of repentance necessary.

Answer

- Who partakes of repentance unto life?

- Who gives repentance unto life?

---

[2] *Divers* meaning diverse.
[3] Titus 3:2–5.
[4] Ecclesiastes 7:20.
[5] *Covenant of Grace* see footnote 4 of chapter 7.
[6] Luke 22:31, 32.
[7] Zechariah 12:10; Acts 11:18.
[8] Ezekiel 36:31; 2 Corinthians 7:11.
[9] Psalm 119:6, 128.
[10] Luke 19:8; 1 Timothy 1:13, 15.
[11] Romans 6:23.
[12] Isaiah 1:16–18; 55:7.

Of Repentance Unto Life and Salvation

- What is its connection with effectual calling?

- What type of people have been mercifully provided repentance unto life?

- Is repentance unto life a grace/gift? If so, what person of the Godhead brings it about?

- What is included in repentance unto life? (Put paragraph 3 into your own words)

- Why is repentance to be continued throughout all of life?

- Of what should we repent?

- What does even the smallest sin deserve?

- What does God give, even to those who commit the greatest of sin, if they repent?

- Why should there be the constant preaching of repentance?

Chapter 16
Of Good Works

Part 1: Bible Study (James 2:14–26)

Read
- Read the passage multiple times.
- Read the passage in a few different translations.
- Take note of what is similar and what is different.

Context
- What sort of writing is this passage: a letter, narrative, poem, wisdom literature, and/or prophecy?
- Who wrote this book? How do you know?
- Who was he writing the letter to? What can you learn about them and the situation of the letter?
- What comes immediately before this passage? Are there any clues to the connection between the text under consideration and that which comes before it?
- What comes immediately after this passage? Are there any clues to the connection between the text under consideration and that which comes after it?

Observation
- Are there any significant divisions or subpoints within the text?
- Are there any connecting words that help us trace the argument? (for, but, therefore, because)
- What is the main point or points?
- What surprises are there? What are some things you don't understand?

Confessing Sound Words

- What are the keywords? What words or ideas are repeated?

Meaning
- How does this passage relate to other parts later in the book?

- Does this passage say anything about Jesus? If so, what?

- What does this teach us about God?

- What does this passage say about us and our salvation?

- How could we sum up the meaning of this passage in our own words?

Application
- What are some differences between you and the original audience?

- How does this passage challenge or confirm your understanding?

- Does this passage and the truth within it call for a particular attitude or posture? If so, what? Is there some attitude you need to change?

- How does this passage call on you to live?

- What does this passage teach you about good works?

Part 2: Scripture Memory (James 2:17; Ephesians 2:8–10)
Putting James into context: Refer to your inductive Bible study.
- Read James 2:14–26.

- What is the fruit of true living faith?

- What are good works? What are some examples?

- How do we know a work is good or not? What is our source to text the goodness of works?

Of Good Works

- Consider the doctrine of justification by faith alone. Does this text contradict the notion that our grounds for justification by God in Christ are the merits of Christ's active and passive obedience (holy life and sacrificial death)? Why or why not?

- What are some good works you can make a regular part of every day and week?

Putting Ephesians 2:8-10 into context: Ephesians is a summary of the gospel. The Triune God accomplishes salvation that the Father plans, the Son executes, and the Spirit applies (1:3-14). It prompts prayer (1:15-23; 3:13-21). This salvation manifests in the life of individuals dead in Sin made alive in Christ by grace through faith (2:1-10). It has corporate and cosmic effects that are revealed in history (2:11-3:13). The salvation God has accomplished by grace through faith works itself out in the lives of those who experience it (4:1-5:17), affecting every relationship (5:18-6:9) and calling them to arms against the forces of darkness (6:10-20). The nature of salvation and its effects in the life of the believer.

- Read Ephesians 2:1-10.

- What is the nature of salvation: grace or works?

- How do we receive the salvation that is completely of grace?

- Is this your own doing? Why or why not?

- What is the relationship between salvation by grace alone and good works?

- How does union with Jesus necessarily entail good works?

- What are some good works God has prepared for you to walk in them?

Part 3: Confession
Read

1. Good works are only such as God has commanded in his Holy Word,[1] and not such as without the warrant thereof are devised by men out of blind zeal, or upon any pretense of good intentions.[2]

2. These good works, done in obedience to God's commandments, are the fruits and evidences of a true and lively faith;[3] and by them believers manifest their thankfulness,[4] strengthen their assurance,[5] edify their brethren, adorn the profession of the gospel,[6] stop the mouths of the adversaries, and glorify God,[7] whose workmanship they are, created in Christ Jesus thereunto,[8] that having their fruit unto holiness they may have the end eternal life.[9]

3. Their ability to do good works is not at all of themselves, but wholly from the Spirit of Christ;[10] and that they may be enabled thereunto, besides the graces they have already received, there is necessary an actual influence of the same Holy Spirit, to work in them to will and to do of his good pleasure;[11] yet they are not hereupon to grow negligent, as if they were not bound to perform any duty, unless upon a special motion of the Spirit, but they ought to be diligent in stirring up the grace of God that is in them.[12]

4. They who in their obedience attain to the greatest height which is possible in this life, are so far from being able to supererogate,[13] and to do more than God requires, as that they fall short of much which in duty they are bound to do.[14]

5. We cannot by our best works merit pardon of sin or eternal life at the hand of God, by reason of the great disproportion that is between them and the glory to come, and the infinite distance that is between us and God, whom by them we can neither profit nor satisfy for the debt of our former sins;[15] but when we have done

---

[1] Micah 6:8; Hebrews 13:21.
[2] Isaiah 29:13; Matthew 15:9.
[3] James 2:18, 22.
[4] Psalm 116:12, 13 .
[5] 2 Peter 1:5-11; 1 John 2:3, 5.
[6] Matthew 5:16.
[7] Philippians 1:11; 1 Timothy 6:1; 1 Peter 2:15.
[8] Ephesians 2:10.
[9] Romans 6:22.
[10] John 15:4, 5.
[11] 2 Corinthians 3:5; Philippians 2:13.
[12] Isaiah 64:7; Philippians 2:12; Hebrews 6:11, 12.
[13] *Supererogate* meaning going beyond our duty.
[14] Job 9:2, 3; Luke 17:10; Galatians 5:17.
[15] Romans 3:20; Ephesians 2:8, 9.

Of Good Works

all we can, we have done but our duty, and are unprofitable servants; and because as they are good they proceed from his Spirit,[16] and as they are wrought by us they are defiled and mixed with so much weakness and imperfection, that they cannot endure the severity of God's punishment.[17] (;;)

6. Yet notwithstanding[18] the persons of believers being accepted through Christ, their good works also are accepted in him;[19] not as though they were in this life wholly unblameable and unreprovable in God's sight, but that he, looking upon them in his Son, is pleased to accept and reward that which is sincere, although accompanied with many weaknesses and imperfections.[20]

7. Works done by unregenerate men, although for the matter of them they may be things which God commands, and of good use both to themselves and others;[21] yet because they proceed not from a heart purified by faith,[22] nor are done in a right manner according to the word,[23] nor to a right end, the glory of God,[24] they are therefore sinful, and cannot please God, nor make a man meet[25] to receive grace from God,[26] and yet their neglect of them is more sinful and displeasing to God.[27]

Answer

- What are good works? What is our source of knowing good works?

- What are not good works? What is not our source of knowing good works?

- What is the relationship between lively faith and good works?

- What effects/benefits will good works have?

- Who is the source or power behind our performing good works?

- Does this mean we should wait for the prompting of the Spirit to perform good works?

---

[16] Romans 4:6; Galatians 5:22, 23.
[17] Psalm 143:2; Isaiah 64:6.
[18] *Notwithstanding* meaning nevertheless or all the same.
[19] Ephesians 1:6; 1 Peter 2:5.
[20] Matthew 25:21, 23; Hebrews 6:10.
[21] 1 Kings 21:27, 29; 2 Kings 10:30.
[22] Genesis 4:5; Hebrews 11:4, 6.
[23] 1 Corinthians 13:1.
[24] Matthew 6:2, 5.
[25] *Meet* meaning suitable or fit.
[26] Amos 5:21, 22; Romans 9:16; Titus 3:5.
[27] Job 21:14, 15; Matthew 25:41–43.

Confessing Sound Words

- What does the confession mean when it says, "they ought to be diligent in stirring up the grace of God that is in them?" What are some ways we can stir up the grace of God within us?

- What can we not accomplish through good works? Why?

- How does our union with Christ impact the way that God views and accepts our good works?

- Can unregenerate man perform good works?

- Why can the good works of unregenerate men not make men suitable to receive God's grace?

- Should unregenerate men still do what God requires even if it does not merit them salvation?

- What will you strive to do this week and coming weeks to stir up God's grace in you?

- What are some good works you have neglected recently?

- What are some good works you will give yourself to?

Chapter 17
Of the Perseverance of the Saints

Part 1: Catechism (Q39)

Q39. What are the benefits in this life that flow from justification, adoption, and sanctification?

The benefits in this life that flow from justification, adoption, and sanctification are assurance of God's love, peace of conscience, joy in the Holy Spirit, increase of grace, and perseverance therein to the end.[1]

- Read all Scripture references.

- What is meant by assurance of God's love?

- What is meant by peace of conscience?

- What is meant by joy in the Holy Spirit?

- What is meant by increase of grace?

- What is meant by perseverance therein to the end?

- How are these benefits related to justification, adoption, and sanctification?

- Have you experienced these blessings in your own life? Give some examples.

Part 2: Bible Study (John 10:22-42)

Read

- Read the passage multiple times.

- Read the passage in a few different translations.

- Take note of what is similar and what is different.

Context

- What sort of writing is this passage: a letter, narrative, poem, wisdom

---

[1] Proverbs 4:18; Romans 5:1, 2, 5, 17; 1 Peter 1:5; 1 John 5:13.

literature, and/or prophecy?

- What has happened so far? What notable characters have been introduced, and what significant events have taken place?

- What is before and after this passage?

- Are there any persons or places that are mentioned that you don't know? (Search them out earlier in the book or with a commentary)

Observation
- Who are the main characters? What do you learn about them?

- Is there any dialogue or speaking? Who speaks? What do they say?

- What is the main point or points?

- What surprises are there? What are some things you don't understand?

- What are the keywords? What words or ideas are repeated?

Meaning
- Does the author provide any commentary for the event? How does this help us understand the story?

- Is any behaviour commended or portrayed as positive? Is any behaviour rebuked or negatively portrayed?

- What does this passage teach us about Jesus (His Person and Work)?

- What does this teach us about God?

- How could we sum up the meaning of this passage in our own words?

Application
- What are some differences between you and the original audience?

Of the Perseverance of the Saints

- How does this passage challenge or confirm my understanding?

- Is there some attitude you need to change?

- What does this passage teach about being one of Jesus' disciples?

- What does this passage teach us about the perseverance of the saints?

Part 3: Scripture Memory (John 10:28, 29; Philippians 1:6)
Putting John 10:28, 29 into context: Refer to your Bible study above.
- Read John 10:22–42.

- Why do some not believe according to Jesus? What differentiates them from those that do? (See John 10:26, 27)

- What is certain for those who are Jesus' sheep? Why is it certain?

- What does God being triune have to do with the doctrine of perseverance?

- Why is the notion of not being plucked from Jesus' and the Father's hand a great comfort? Who alone can enjoy such comfort?

Putting Philippians 1:6 into context: Philippians is a letter containing much thanksgiving and joy. Philippians 1:6 comes amid Paul's thanksgiving and petitions for the Philippian church.
- Read Philippians 1:3–11.

- Of what is Paul sure?

- What is the good work God has begun?

- When will it be brought to completion?

- In what ways should and does this passage provide encouragement for you on this side of glory?

Confessing Sound Words

Part 4: Confession

Read

1. Those whom God has accepted in the beloved, effectually called and sanctified by his Spirit, and given the precious faith of his elect unto, can neither totally nor finally fall from the state of grace, but shall certainly persevere therein to the end, and be eternally saved, seeing the gifts and callings of God are without repentance, whence[2] he still begets and nourishes in them faith, repentance, love, joy, hope, and all the graces of the Spirit unto immortality;[3] and though many storms and floods arise and beat against them, yet they shall never be able to take them off that foundation and rock which by faith they are fastened upon; notwithstanding,[4] through unbelief and the temptations of Satan, the sensible sight of the light and love of God may for a time be clouded and obscured from them,[5] yet he is still the same, and they shall be sure to be kept by the power of God unto salvation, where they shall enjoy their purchased possession, they being engraven[6] upon the palm of his hands, and their names having been written in the book of life from all eternity.[7]

2. This perseverance of the saints depends not upon their own free will, but upon the immutability of the decree of election,[8] flowing from the free and unchangeable love of God the Father, upon the efficacy of the merit and intercession of Jesus Christ and union with him,[9] the oath of God,[10] the abiding of his Spirit, and the seed of God within them,[11] and the nature of the covenant of grace;[12] [13] from all which arises also the certainty and infallibility thereof.

3. And though they may, through the temptation of Satan and of the world, the prevalency of corruption remaining in them, and the neglect of means of their preservation, fall into grievous sins, and for a time continue therein,[14] whereby they incur God's displeasure and grieve his Holy Spirit,[15] come to have their graces and

---

[2] *Whence* meaning out of which or from which.
[3] John 10:28, 29; Philippians 1:6; 2 Timothy 2:19; 1 John 2:19.
[4] *Notwithstanding* meaning nevertheless or all the same.
[5] Psalm 89:31, 32; 1 Corinthians 11:32.
[6] *Engraven* meaning engraved.
[7] Malachi 3:6.
[8] Romans 8:30; 9:11, 16.
[9] John 14:19; Romans 5:9, 10.
[10] Hebrews 6:17, 18.
[11] 1 John 3:9.
[12] Jeremiah 32:40.
[13] *Covenant of Grace* see footnote 4 of chapter 7.
[14] Matthew 26:70, 72, 74.
[15] Isaiah 64:5, 9; Ephesians 4:30.

comforts impaired,[16] have their hearts hardened, and their consciences wounded,[17] hurt and scandalize others, and bring temporal judgements upon themselves,[18] yet shall they renew their repentance and be preserved through faith in Christ Jesus to the end.[19]

Answer

- Who experiences the benefit of the perseverance of the saints?

- What does the perseverance of the saints entail? What are the aspects of perseverance of the saints?

- What are the grounds for or is the foundation of perseverance of the saints?

- How does God accomplish the perseverance of the saints in the believer?

- On what does perseverance depend?

- On what does perseverance not depend?

- Though saints persevere in the end, what might saints fall into this side of glory?

- How does a saint fall into such a state?

- What will happen to them in the end?

- What are some applications and implications of the doctrine of the perseverance of the saints in the life of the believer?

---

[16] Psalm 51:10, 12.
[17] Psalm 32:3, 4.
[18] 2 Samuel 12:14.
[19] Luke 22:32, 61, 62.

Chapter 18
Of the Assurance of Grace and Salvation

Part 1: Bible Study (2 Peter 1:3–11)
Read
- Read the passage multiple times.

- Read the passage in a few different translations.

- Take note of what is similar and what is different.

Context
- What sort of writing is this passage: a letter, narrative, poem, wisdom literature, and/or prophecy?

- Who wrote this book? How do you know?

- Who was he writing the letter to? What can you learn about them and the situation of the letter?

- What comes immediately before this passage? Are there any clues to the connection between the text under consideration and that which comes before it?

- What comes immediately after this passage? Are there any clues to the connection between the text under consideration and that which comes after it?

Observation
- Are there any significant divisions or subpoints within the text?

- Are there any connecting words that help us trace the argument? (for, but, therefore, because)

- What is the main point or points?

- What surprises are there? What are some things you don't understand?

Confessing Sound Words

- What are the keywords? What words or ideas are repeated?

Meaning
- How does this passage relate to other parts later in the book?
- Does this passage say anything about Jesus? If so, what?
- What does this teach us about God?
- What does this passage say about us and our salvation?
- How could we sum up the meaning of this passage in our own words?

Application
- What are some differences between you and the original audience?
- How does this passage challenge or confirm your understanding?
- Does this passage and the truth within it call for a particular attitude or posture? If so, what? Is there some attitude you need to change?
- How does this passage call on you to live?
- What does this passage teach you about the assurance of grace and salvation?

Part 2: Scripture Memory (1 John 5:12, 13; Hebrews 6:11, 12)

Putting 1 John 5:12, 13 into context: 1 John is the first of three letters written by the apostle John. In this letter, he refutes false teachers and gives Christians different tests to check the legitimacy of our communion with God. In doing so, He drives us to 1) analyze the fruit of teachers before we listen to them and 2) to Christ as the ground and rock of our assurance. The memory verses memorize the second point.
- Read 1 John 5:6–21
- Who has life?
- Who does not have life?

Of the Assurance of Grace and Salvation

- What does life mean in this context?

- Why did John write this letter?

- Who may know that they have eternal life?

- What or who is the ground of our assurance of salvation?

Putting Hebrews 6:11, 12 into context: Hebrews is a theologically dense book in which the necessity of sticking with Jesus regardless of circumstances is pressed upon the reader repeatedly. The author, who many until recently thought was Paul, grounds this charge to stick with Jesus in a rich Christology (Doctrine of Christ). Jesus is first, final, faithful, and fatal. He is God the Son incarnate. He is a prophet, priest, and king, who teaches, represents, rules his people. Our memory concludes a warning passage. The warning is do not leave Jesus. Assurance comes from union with Christ (6:19, 20).
- Read Hebrews 5:11–6:20

- What does the author of Hebrews desire for his readers?

- Why does he desire this for the readers?

- Does assurance of salvation promote sinful living for the Christian? Why or why not?

Part 3: Confession
Read

1. Although temporary believers, and other unregenerate men, may vainly deceive themselves with false hopes and carnal presumptions of being in the favour of God and state of salvation, which hope of theirs shall perish;[1] yet such as truly believe in the Lord Jesus, and love him in sincerity, endeavoring to walk in all good conscience before him, may in this life be certainly assured that they are in the state

---

[1] Job 8:13, 14; Matthew 7:22, 23.

of grace, and may rejoice in the hope of the glory of God,[2] which hope shall never make them ashamed.[3]

2. This certainty is not a bare conjectural and probable persuasion grounded upon a fallible hope, but an infallible assurance of faith,[4] founded on the blood and righteousness of Christ revealed in the Gospel;[5] and also upon the inward evidence of those graces of the Spirit unto which promises are made,[6] and on the testimony of the Spirit of adoption, witnessing with our spirits that we are the children of God;[7] and, as a fruit thereof, keeping the heart both humble and holy.[8]

3. This infallible assurance does not so belong to the essence of faith, but that a true believer may wait long, and conflict with many difficulties before he be partaker of it;[9] yet being enabled by the Spirit to know the things which are freely given him of God, he may, without extraordinary revelation, in the right use of means, attain thereunto:[10] and therefore it is the duty of every one to give all diligence to make his calling and election sure, that thereby his heart may be enlarged in peace and joy in the Holy Spirit, in love and thankfulness to God, and in strength and cheerfulness in the duties of obedience, the proper fruits of this assurance;[11]—so far is it from inclining men to looseness.[12]

4. True believers may have the assurance of their salvation divers[13] ways shaken, diminished, and intermitted;[14] as by negligence in preserving of it,[15] by falling into some special sin which wound the conscience and grieve the Spirit;[16] by some sudden or vehement[17] temptation,[18] by God's withdrawing the light of his countenance, and suffering even such as fear him to walk in darkness and to have no light,[19] yet

---

[2] 1 John 2:3; 3:14, 18, 19, 21, 24; 5:13.
[3] Romans 5:2, 5.
[4] Hebrews 6:11, 19.
[5] Hebrews 6:17, 18.
[6] 2 Peter 1:4, 5, 10, 11.
[7] Romans 8:15, 16.
[8] 1 John 3:1-3.
[9] Psalm 77:1-12; 88; Isaiah 50:10.
[10] Hebrews 6:11, 12; 1 John 4:13.
[11] Psalm 119:32; Romans 5:1, 2, 5; 14:17.
[12] Romans 6:1, 2; Titus 2:11, 12, 14.
[13] *Divers* meaning diverse.
[14] *Intermitted* meaning interrupted.
[15] Song of Solomon 5:2-3, 6.
[16] Psalm 51:8, 12, 14.
[17] *Vehement* meaning extremely strong.
[18] Psalm 31:22; 77:7, 8; 116:11.
[19] Psalm 30:7.

Of the Assurance of Grace and Salvation

are they never destitute of the seed of God[20] and life of faith,[21] that love of Christ and the brethren, that sincerity of heart and conscience of duty out of which, by the operation of the Spirit, this assurance may in due time be revived,[22] and by the which, in the meantime, they are preserved from utter despair.[23]

Answer

- What might temporary believers experience? Will this experience continue?

- Who may experience assurance that they are in the state of grace?

- What is the nature of this assurance?

- What is assurance founded upon?

- What is the Spirit's role in assurance?

- What is the relationship between assurance and faith? Will all who have true faith experience assurance?

- How may a believer acquire assurance? What might he or she use?

- What is the duty of everyone?

- Why should everyone give themselves to this duty?

- What might happen to a believer's assurance?

- How does this happen?

- What is a believer never without?

- Have you ever lacked assurance of salvation? If so, what was it like? How did it come back?

- What are the ordinary means we might give ourselves to so that we may have assurance?

---

[20] 1 John 3:9.
[21] Luke 22:32.
[22] Psalm 42:5, 11.
[23] Lamentations 3:26–31.

Chapter 19
Of the Law of God

Catechism (Q44–47)

Q44. What is the duty which God requires of man?
The duty which God requires of man is obedience to his revealed will.[1]
- Read all Scripture references.

- What is God's revealed will?

- Where can we find God's revealed will?

- How is God's revealed will distinct from his hidden will?

Q45. What did God at first reveal to man for the rule of his obedience?
The rule which God at first revealed to man for his obedience was the moral law.[2]
- Read all Scripture references.

- What does the term moral mean?

- When did God reveal this moral law to man?

- Who has access to this revelation?

Q46. Where is the moral law summarized?
The moral law is summarized in the ten commandments.[3]
- Read all Scripture references.

- What are the ten commandments?

---

[1] 1 Samuel 15:22; Micah 6:8.
[2] Romans 2:14, 15; 10:5.
[3] Deuteronomy 10:4; Matthew 19:17–19.

Confessing Sound Words

Q47. What is the sum of the ten commandments?

The sum of the ten commandments is to love the Lord our God, with all our heart, with all our soul, with all our strength, and with all our mind; and our neighbor as ourselves.[4]

- Read all Scripture references.

- How do the ten commandments fit within the two great commandments?

- What are some ways you can express love to God?

- What are some ways you can express love to your neighbour?

Bible Study (Exodus 20:1–21)
Read
- Read the passage multiple times.

- Read the passage in a few different translations.

- Take note of what is similar and what is different.

Context
- What type of literature is the passage? (Is it narrative, a gospel, prophecy, poetry, or something else?)

- What has happened so far in the story?

- What happened immediately before this passage? How do you think this passage and the one before it are connected?

- What comes immediately after this story?

---

[4] Matthew 22:37–40.

Observation
- Who are the main characters in the story? What are we told about them?
- Where do the events in the story take place?
- Is there a problem in the story that needs resolution?
- What is the main point of the story or theme in the story?
- Is there anything that surprised or confused you?

Meaning
- Does the narrator of the story provide any commentary? If so, what does he say? How does this help give us clarity in what is being told to us?
- Does anyone in the story learn something? Are they given a new command? If so, what did they learn? What were they commanded to do?
- Are there any threats made? What are they?
- Are there any promises made? What are they?
- Is this story taken up thematically, alluded to, or quoted elsewhere in the Bible? If so, what is said?
- How does this passage point to Jesus or find its ultimate fulfillment in him?
- Summarize the meaning or big idea(s) of this passage in your own words.

Application
- What does this passage call you to believe about God?
- What does this passage call you to do? What attitude or behaviour do you need to change?
- What does this passage teach us about the law of God?

Confessing Sound Words

Scripture Memory (Matthew 22:37-39; Romans 3:20)
Putting Matthew 22:37-39 into context: The contents of these verses are Jesus' response to a question from the Pharisees. They had just witnessed him silence the Sadducees about the resurrection. Now they hoped to silence Jesus.
- Read Matthew 22:23–40

- How do the ten commandments fit within these two great commandments?

- What is the first great commandment?

- What is the second great commandment?

- What is meant by verse 40?

- What are tangible ways you can love God and neighbour this week?

Putting Romans 3:20 into context: Romans is the longest letter of the apostle Paul. Romans 1:16, 17 teaches revelation of God's righteousness in the Gospel. Romans 1:18–3:20 teaches the universal unrighteousness of humanity. Our verse focuses in on the inadequacy of the law to make sinners righteous.
- Read Romans 3:1–26.

- Is the law flawed? Why or why not?

- What can the law not do?

- What does the law do?

- How is a sinner justified?

- Does the law have any function in the justified believer's life?

Of the Law of God

Confession

Read

1. God gave to Adam a law of universal obedience[5] written in his heart, and a particular precept[6] of not eating the fruit of the tree of knowledge of good and evil;[7] by which he bound him and all his posterity to personal, entire, exact, and perpetual obedience;[8] promised life upon the fulfilling, and threatened death upon the breach of it, and endued him with power and ability to keep it.[9]

2. The same law that was first written in the heart of man continued to be a perfect rule of righteousness after the fall,[10] and was delivered by God upon Mount Sinai, in ten commandments, and written in two tables, the four first containing our duty towards God, and the other six, our duty to man.[11]

3. Besides this law, commonly called moral, God was pleased to give to the people of Israel ceremonial laws, containing several typical ordinances, partly of worship, prefiguring Christ, his graces, actions, sufferings, and benefits;[12] and partly holding forth divers[13] instructions of moral duties,[14] all which ceremonial laws being appointed only to the time of reformation, are, by Jesus Christ the true Messiah and only law-giver, who was furnished with power from the Father for that end abrogated and taken away.[15]

4. To them also he gave sundry[16] judicial laws, which expired together with the state of that people, not obliging any now by virtue of that institution; their general equity only being of moral use.[17]

5. The moral law does forever bind all, as well justified persons as others, to the obedience thereof,[18] and that not only in regard of the matter contained in it, but also in respect of the authority of God the Creator, who gave it;[19] neither does Christ in the Gospel any way dissolve, but much strengthen this obligation.[20]

---

[5] See footnote 35 of chapter 2.
[6] See footnote 35 of chapter 2.
[7] Genesis 1:27; Ecclesiastes 7:29
[8] Romans 10:5.
[9] Galatians 3:10, 12.
[10] Romans 2:14, 15.
[11] Deuteronomy 10:4.
[12] Colossians 2:17; Hebrews 10:1.
[13] *Divers* meaning diverse.
[14] 1 Corinthians 5:7
[15] Ephesians 2:14, 16; Colossians 2:14, 16, 17.
[16] *Sundry* meaning various.
[17] 1 Corinthians 9:8–10.
[18] Romans 13:8–10; James 2:8, 10–12.
[19] James 2:10, 11.
[20] Matthew 5:17–19; Romans 3:31.

6. Although true believers be not under the law as a covenant of works, to be thereby justified or condemned,[21] yet it is of great use to them as well as to others, in that as a rule of life, informing them of the will of God and their duty, it directs and binds them to walk accordingly; discovering also the sinful pollutions of their natures, hearts, and lives, so as examining themselves thereby, they may come to further conviction of, humiliation for, and hatred against, sin;[22] together with a clearer sight of the need they have of Christ and the perfection of his obedience; it is likewise of use to the regenerate to restrain their corruptions, in that it forbids sin; and the threatenings of it serve to shew what even their sins deserve, and what afflictions in this life they may expect for them, although freed from the curse and unallayed rigour thereof. The promises of it likewise shows them God's approbation[23] of obedience, and what blessings they may expect upon the performance thereof, though not as due to them by the law as a covenant of works; so as man's doing good and refraining from evil, because the law encourages to the one and deters from the other, is no evidence of his being under the law and not under grace.[24]

7. Neither are the aforementioned uses of the law contrary to the grace of the Gospel, but do sweetly comply with it,[25] the Spirit of Christ subduing and enabling the will of man to do that freely and cheerfully which the will of God, revealed in the law, requires to be done.[26]

Answer

- What law was given to Adam? What two types of laws were given to Adam? How do they differ?

- What law is on the heart of everyone even after the fall?

- Where do we find a summary of this law?

- What additional laws did God give Israel? What was their function? What is their bearing upon the Christian?

- In addition to the ceremonial laws and the ten commandments, what other

---

[21] Romans 6:14; 8:1; 10:4; Galatians 2:16.
[22] Romans 3:20; 7:7, etc.
[23] *Approbation* meaning approval.
[24] Romans 6:12-14; 1 Peter 3:8-13.
[25] Galatians 3:21.
[26] Ezekiel 36:27.

laws did God give Israel? What is their application for the present day?

- What is the relationship of the believer to the moral law?

- What could the law not do?

- What are the uses of the law?

- Do these uses contradict the grace of the gospel? Why or why not?

- How does the Confession's understanding of the law help in public debate over laws and morals?

- How can we teach, preach, and enforce the law of God in church without being legalistic?

Chapter 20
Of the Gospel and of the Extent of the Grace Thereof

Part 1: Bible Study (1 Corinthians 15:1–11)
Read
- Read the passage multiple times.
- Read the passage in a few different translations.
- Take note of what is similar and what is different.

Context
- What sort of writing is this passage: a letter, narrative, poem, wisdom literature, and/or prophecy?
- Who wrote this book? How do you know?
- Who was he writing the letter to? What can you learn about them and the situation of the letter?
- What comes immediately before this passage? Are there any clues to the connection between the text under consideration and that which comes before it?
- What comes immediately after this passage? Are there any clues to the connection between the text under consideration and that which comes after it?

Observation
- Are there any significant divisions or subpoints within the text?
- Are there any connecting words that help us trace the argument? (for, but, therefore, because)
- What is the main point or points?
- What surprises are there? What are some things you don't understand?

Confessing Sound Words

- What are the keywords? What words or ideas are repeated?

Meaning
- How does this passage relate to other parts later in the book?

- Does this passage say anything about Jesus? If so, what?

- What does this teach us about God?

- What does this passage say about us and our salvation?

- How could we sum up the meaning of this passage in our own words?

Application
- What are some differences between you and the original audience?

- How does this passage challenge or confirm your understanding?

- Does this passage and the truth within it call for a particular attitude or posture? If so, what? Is there some attitude you need to change?

- How does this passage call on you to live?

- What does this passage teach us about the gospel?

Part 2: Scripture Memory (Gen 3:15; Romans 1:16, 17)
Putting Gen 3:15 in context: This promise of a serpent slaying seed begins the story of redemption that will unfold and culminate in the person and work of the Lord Jesus Christ. It is proclaimed to the serpent after man fell in Adam's sin.
- Read Genesis 3.

- Who is the seed that crushes the serpent's head? How do we know?

- Was Jesus a backup plan? Why or why not?

Of the Gospel and of the Extent of the Grace Thereof

- At this point, what do we know of the promised redeemer?

- How is this theme of a promised seed and redeemer developed and progressively made clearer throughout the Old Testament?

Putting Romans 1:16, 17 in context: As I have written earlier, this is Paul's longest letter. In it, he expounds and applies the gospel of the Lord Jesus Christ. The verses stand as a transition from the initial greeting to the doctrinal section of the book (Romans 1:16–11:36).

- Read Romans 1:1–17.

- You have read, studied, and memorized other passages in Romans. How do these two verses set the stage for what follows?

- Of what is Paul not ashamed?

- Why is Paul not ashamed of it?

- What does it look like for us not to be ashamed of it?

Part 3: Confession
Read

1. The covenant of works[1] being broken by sin, and made unprofitable unto life, God was pleased to give forth the promise of Christ, the seed of the woman, as the means of calling the elect, and begetting in them faith and repentance;[2] in this promise the gospel, as to the substance of it, was revealed, and therein effectual for the conversion and salvation of sinners.[3]

2. This promise of Christ, and salvation by him, is revealed only by the Word of God;[4] neither do the works of creation or providence, with the light of nature, make discovery of Christ, or of grace by him, so much as in a general or obscure way;[5]

---

[1] *Covenant of works* see footnote 3 of chapter 7.
[2] Genesis 3:15.
[3] Revelation 13:8.
[4] Romans 1:17.
[5] Romans 10:14, 15, 17.

Confessing Sound Words

much less that men destitute of the revelation of Him by the promise or gospel, should be enabled thereby to attain saving faith or repentance.[6]

3. The revelation of the gospel unto sinners, made in divers[7] times and by sundry[8] parts, with the addition of promises and precepts for the obedience required therein, as to the nations and persons to whom it is granted, is merely of the sovereign will and good pleasure of God;[9] not being annexed[10] by virtue of any promise to the due improvement of men's natural abilities, by virtue of common light received without it, which none ever did make, or can do so;[11] and therefore in all ages, the preaching of the gospel has been granted unto persons and nations, as to the extent or straitening of it, in great variety, according to the counsel of the will of God.

4. Although the gospel be the only outward means of revealing Christ and saving grace, and is, as such, abundantly sufficient thereunto; yet that men who are dead in trespasses may be born again, quickened or regenerated, there is moreover necessary an effectual insuperable[12] work of the Holy Spirit upon the whole soul, for the producing in them a new spiritual life;[13] without which no other means will effect their conversion unto God.[14]

Answer

- What was broken by sin and could not profit life?

- What did God give that could profit life to the elect?

- Where was it first given?

- How were the elect before the coming of Christ saved?

- Where is the promise of Christ and salvation by him revealed?

- Where is it not revealed?

---

[6] Proverbs 29:18; Isaiah 25:7; 60:2, 3.
[7] *Divers* meaning diverse.
[8] *Sundry* meaning various.
[9] Psalm 147:20; Acts 16:7.
[10] *Annexed* meaning to join or attach.
[11] Romans 1:18-32.
[12] *Insuperable* meaning unable to overcome or unconquerable.
[13] Psalm 110:3; 1 Corinthians 2:14; Ephesians 1:19, 20.
[14] John 6:44; 2 Corinthians 4:4, 6.

Of the Gospel and of the Extent of the Grace Thereof

- Are those who do not receive this special revelation able to know and believe in Christ? Why or why not?

- What alone has God chosen to use to save sinners?

- What cannot be used to save sinners?

- What is the gospel sufficient to do?

- What also is necessary to apply the gospel to the heart of the dead sinner?

- If what this chapter communicates is true, what should be central in all the ministries of the church?

- Since the gospel is God's only ordained means of saving sinners that he effectually applies to his elect, why should we be bold in sharing it with our unconverted neighbours?

Chapter 21
Of Christian Liberty and Liberty of Conscience

Part 1: Bible Study (2 Corinthians 3:1–18)

Read
- Read the passage multiple times.

- Read the passage in a few different translations.

- Take note of what is similar and what is different.

Context
- What sort of writing is this passage: a letter, narrative, poem, wisdom literature, and/or prophecy?

- Who wrote this book? How do you know?

- Who was he writing the letter to? What can you learn about them and the situation of the letter?

- What comes immediately before this passage? Are there any clues to the connection between the text under consideration and that which comes before it?

- What comes immediately after this passage? Are there any clues to the connection between the text under consideration and that which comes after it?

Observation
- Are there any significant divisions or subpoints within the text?

- Are there any connecting words that help us trace the argument? (for, but, therefore, because)

- What is the main point or points?

- What surprises are there? What are some things you don't understand?

Confessing Sound Words

- What are the keywords? What words or ideas are repeated?

Meaning
- How does this passage relate to other parts later in the book?
- Does this passage say anything about Jesus? If so, what?
- What does this teach us about God?
- What does this passage say about us and our salvation?
- How could we sum up the meaning of this passage in our own words?

Application
- What are some differences between you and the original audience?
- How does this passage challenge or confirm your understanding?
- Does this passage and the truth within it call for a particular attitude or posture? If so, what? Is there some attitude you need to change?
- How does this passage call on you to live?
- What does this passage teach us about Christian liberty or liberty of conscience?

Part 2: Scripture Memory (Gal 3:13, 14; James 4:12)
Putting Galatians 3:13, 14 into context: Paul wrote this letter to a group of churches located near modern-day Turkey. He has proclaimed the gospel in these churches. This letter's purpose was to call them back to the gospel and refute the errors of those who would lead these churches away from it. There is only one gospel (Galatians 1:6–9), the gospel of free grace in Christ. Paul defends his apostolic authority in chapters one and two. He defends and explains the notion that all who place faith in Jesus partake of His salvation regardless of ethnicity in chapters 3 and 4. Indeed, the Christ has redeemed them from the "rigour and curse of the law" (2LBCF 21.1)

Of Christian Liberty and Liberty of Conscience

- Read Galatians 3:10-14.

- What cannot justify a person?

- Why are those who rely on the works of the law under a curse?

- In what way does Jesus free us from the law?

- How did Jesus do this?

- How do we receive the promised Spirit?

Putting James 4:12 into context: James, the brother of Jesus, provides guidance to Christians to live in wise obedience to their Lord. They must persevere (1:1-26), have living faith (2:1-26), watch their tongue (3:1-12), embody heavenly wisdom (3:13-18), submit to God's will (4:1-5:6), and be patient (5:7-20). The memory verse gives ground to the command not to slander fellow Christians (4:11). There is only one true judge, and it is not you.

- Read James 4:1-12.

- Who alone is the lawgiver and judge?

- How does this verse convey the idea that God alone is the Lord of the conscience?

- How does this verse support the command in verse 11?

Part 3: Confession
Read

1. The liberty which Christ has purchased for believers under the gospel, consists in their freedom from the guilt of sin, the condemning wrath of God, the rigor and curse of the law,[1] and in their being delivered from this present evil world,[2]

---

[1] Galatians 3:13.
[2] Galatians 1:4.

bondage to Satan,³ and dominion of sin,⁴ from the evil of afflictions,⁵ the fear and sting of death, the victory of the grave,⁶ and ever-lasting damnation:⁷ as also in their free access to God, and their yielding obedience unto Him, not out of slavish fear,⁸ but a child-like love and willing mind.⁹

All which were common also to believers under the law for the substance of them;¹⁰ but under the New Testament the liberty of Christians is further enlarged, in their freedom from the yoke of a ceremonial law,¹¹ to which the Jewish church was subjected, and in greater boldness of access to the throne of grace, and in fuller communications of the free Spirit of God, than believers under the law did ordinarily partake of.¹²

2. God alone is Lord of the conscience,¹³ and has left it free from the doctrines and commandments of men which are in anything contrary to his word, or not contained in it.¹⁴ So that to believe such doctrines, or obey such commands out of conscience, is to betray true liberty of conscience;¹⁵ and the requiring of an implicit faith, an absolute and blind obedience, is to destroy liberty of conscience and reason also.¹⁶

3. They who upon pretense of Christian liberty do practice any sin, or cherish any sinful lust, as they do thereby pervert the main design of the grace of the gospel to their own destruction,¹⁷ so they wholly destroy the end of Christian liberty, which is, that being delivered out of the hands of all our enemies, we might serve the Lord without fear, in holiness and righteousness before him, all the days of our lives.¹⁸

---

³ Acts 26:18.
⁴ Romans 8:3.
⁵ Romans 8:28.
⁶ 1 Corinthians 15:54-57.
⁷ 2 Thessalonians 1:10.
⁸ Romans 8:15.
⁹ Luke 1:73-75; 1 John 4:18.
¹⁰ Galatians 3:9, 14.
¹¹ *Ceremonial Law* meaning those positive laws (see foot note 6 of chapter 2) given to Israel regarding the sacrifices, festivals, rituals, and priest hood they were to perform as God's consecrated people under the Old Covenant. These ceremonies prefigured the person and work of Christ. Keeping these laws were required for their continuance in the land of Canaan.
¹² John 7:38, 39; Hebrews 10:19-21.
¹³ Romans 14:4; James 4:12.
¹⁴ Matthew 15:9; Acts 4:19, 29; 1 Corinthians 7:23.
¹⁵ Colossians 2:20, 22, 23.
¹⁶ 1 Corinthians 3:5; 2 Corinthians 1:24.
¹⁷ Romans 6:1, 2.
¹⁸ Galatians 5:13; 2 Peter 2:18, 21.

Of Christian Liberty and Liberty of Conscience

Answer

- Of what does Christian liberty consist? From what have Christians gained liberty?

- How does Christian liberty differ under the New Covenant?

- Who alone is the Lord of the conscience?

- What does this give the Christian freedom from?

- Does the doctrine of Christian liberty permit sinful living among Christians? Why or why not?

- Have you ever tried to be the Lord of conscience for another Christian? If so, explain. If not, explain what this would look like.

- Have you ever abused the notion of Christian liberty to permit sin? If so, explain. If not, explain what this would look like.

- Summarize the doctrine of Christian liberty in your own words.

Chapter 22
Of Religious Worship and the Sabbath Day

Part 1: Catechism (Q62–67)

Q62. What is the fourth commandment?

The fourth commandment is "Remember the Sabbath day, to keep it holy. Six days you shall labour, and do all your work, but the seventh day is a Sabbath to the LORD your God. On it, you shall not do any work, you, or your son, or your daughter, your male servant, or your female servant, or your livestock, or the sojourner who is within your gates. For in six days, the LORD made heaven and earth, the sea, and all that is in them, and rested on the seventh day. Therefore the LORD blessed the Sabbath day and made it holy."[1]

- Summarize this commandment in your own words.

Q63. What is required in the fourth commandment?

The fourth commandment requires keeping one whole day holy in seven as a sabbath to him.[2]

- Read the biblical cited passages.

- What are some challenges to keeping one whole day holy?

Q64. Which day of seven has God appointed to be the weekly sabbath?

Before the resurrection of Christ, God appointed the seventh day of the week to be the weekly sabbath. From after the resurrection to the end of the world, the first day of the week is the Christian sabbath.[3]

- Read the cited passages.

- What event lead to the moving of the sabbath?

- What day is the Christian sabbath?

---

[1] Exodus 20:8–11 ESV.
[2] Exodus 20:8–11; Deuteronomy 5:12–14.
[3] Exodus 20:8–11; Deuteronomy 5:12–14; Psalm 118:24; Matthew 28:1; Mark 2:27, 28; 16:2; Luke 24:1, 30–36; John 20:1, 19–21; Acts 1:3; 2:1, 2; 20:7; 1 Corinthians 16:1, 2.

Q65. How is the sabbath to be sanctified?

The sabbath is to be sanctified by a refraining from worldly employments and recreations lawful on other days. It is also to be spent in the public and private worship of God; the only exceptions are works of necessity and mercy.[4]

- Read the scripture references.

- What are we to refrain from on the sabbath?

- What are you to participate in on the sabbath?

- What exceptions are given?

- What are some specific examples of these exceptions?

Q66. What is forbidden in the fourth commandment?

The fourth commandment forbids the omission or careless performance of required duties. It forbids profaning the day by idleness, by doing that which in and of itself sinful, or by unnecessary thoughts, words, or works, about worldly employments or recreations.[5]

- Read the scripture references.

- What are some examples of omission of required duties?

- What are some examples of careless performance of required duties?

- State the second sentence in your own words.

- Why is it so hard to avoid what is forbidden on the sabbath in our day and age?

Q67. What are the reasons attached to the fourth commandment?

---

[4] Exodus 16:25-28; 20:8, 10; Nehemiah 13:15-22; Psalm 92; Isaiah 66:23; Matthew 12:1-13; Luke 4:16; Acts 10:7.
[5] Isaiah 58:13; Jeremiah 17:24-27; Ezekiel 22:26; 23:38; Amos 8:5; Malachi 1:13; Acts 20:7, 9.

Of Religious Worship and the Sabbath Day

The reasons attached to the fourth commandment are God's allowing us six days of the week for our lawful employments, his taking a special ownership of a seventh, his own example, and his blessing the sabbath day.[6]

- Read the Scripture references.

- What can we do the other six days of the week to ensure that we keep the sabbath?

- How can we encourage others in our church to keep the Christian sabbath?

Part 2: Bible Study (Leviticus 10:1–19)

Read

- Read the passage multiple times.

- Read the passage in a few different translations.

- Take note of what is similar and what is different.

Context

- What type of literature is the passage? (Is it narrative, a gospel, prophecy, poetry, or something else?)

- What has happened so far in the story?

- What happened immediately before this passage? How do you think this passage and the one before it are connected?

- What comes immediately after this story?

Observation

- Who are the main characters in the story? What are we told about them?

- Where do the events in the story take place?

---

[6] Exodus 20:9, 11.

Confessing Sound Words

- Is there a problem in the story that needs resolution?

- What is the main point of the story or theme in the story?

- Is there anything that surprised or confused you?

Meaning
- Does the narrator of the story provide any commentary? If so, what does he say? How does this help give us clarity in what is being told to us?

- Does anyone in the story learn something? Are they given a new command? If so, what did they learn? What were they commanded to do?

- Are there any threats made? What are they?

- Are there any promises made? What are they?

- Is this story taken up thematically, alluded to, or quoted elsewhere in the Bible? If so, what is said?

- How does this passage point to Jesus or find its ultimate fulfillment in him?

- Summarize the meaning or big idea(s) of this passage in your own words.

Application
- What does this passage call you to believe about God?

- What does this passage call you to do? What attitude or behaviour do you need to change?

- What does this passage teach us about religious worship and the sabbath?

Part 3: Scripture Memory (Deuteronomy 12:32; Exodus 20:8-11)

Putting Deuteronomy 12:32 in context: Deuteronomy is the concluding book of the Pentateuch/Torah. It contains three addresses to the generation that would enter and take the land of Canaan. It includes a retelling of what had happened in the prior generation, a retelling of the Ten Commandments, instructions for life in the land, promises of blessing for obedience, and warnings of curses for disobedience. The prior generation with Moses would not enter the promised land due to their sin. This book is Moses' final words to his people.

- Read Deuteronomy 12:29-13:18.

- What shall we be careful to do?

- What must we be careful not to do?

- What are some of the things that God commanded us to do in corporate worship?

- What are some things churches are tempted to add or take away?

Putting Exodus 20:8-11 in context: Review to your Bible study from chapter 19.

- Read Exodus 20:1-21 and Deuteronomy 5:12-15.

- What is the commandment given in the memory verses?

- What other days has God given us to work?

- Why are we to keep this command?

- Have you failed to keep this command? What do you find difficult about keeping it?

Part 4: Confession
Read

1. The light of nature shows that there is a God, who has lordship and sovereignty over all; is just, good and does good unto all; and is therefore to be feared, loved, praised, called upon, trusted in, and served, with all the heart and all the soul,

and with all the might.[7] But the acceptable way of worshipping the true God, is instituted by himself,[8] and so limited by his own revealed will, that he may not be worshipped according to the imagination and devices of men, nor the suggestions of Satan, under any visible representations, or any other way not prescribed in the Holy Scriptures.[9]

2. Religious worship is to be given to God the Father, Son, and Holy Spirit, and to him alone;[10] not to angels, saints, or any other creatures;[11] and since the fall, not without a mediator,[12] nor in the mediation of any other but Christ alone.[13]

3. Prayer, with thanksgiving, being one part of natural worship, is by God required of all men.[14] But that it may be accepted, it is to be made in the name of the Son,[15] by the help of the Spirit,[16] according to his will;[17] with understanding, reverence, humility, fervency, faith, love, and perseverance; and when with others, in a known tongue.[18]

4. Prayer is to be made for things lawful, and for all sorts of men living, or that shall live hereafter;[19] but not for the dead,[20] nor for those of whom it may be known that they have sinned the sin unto death.[21]

5. The reading of the Scriptures,[22] preaching, and hearing the Word of God,[23] teaching and admonishing one another in psalms, hymns, and spiritual songs, singing with grace in our hearts to the Lord;[24] as also the administration of baptism,[25] and the Lord's Supper,[26] are all parts of religious worship of God, to be performed in obedience to him, with understanding, faith, reverence, and godly fear;

---

[7] Jeremiah 10:7; Mark 12:33.
[8] Deuteronomy 12:32.
[9] Exodus 20:4–6.
[10] Matthew 4:9, 10; 28:19; John 6:23.
[11] Romans 1:25; Colossians 2:18; Revelation 19:10.
[12] John 14:6.
[13] 1 Timothy 2:5.
[14] Psalm 65:2; 95:1–7.
[15] John 14:13, 14.
[16] Romans 8:26.
[17] 1 John 5:14.
[18] 1 Corinthians 14:16, 17.
[19] 2 Samuel 7:29; 1 Timothy 2:1, 2.
[20] 2 Samuel 12:21–23.
[21] 1 John 5:16.
[22] 1 Timothy 4:13.
[23] Luke 8:18; 2 Timothy 4:2.
[24] Ephesians 5:19; Colossians 3:16.
[25] Matthew 28:19, 20.
[26] 1 Corinthians 11:26.

Of Religious Worship and the Sabbath Day

moreover, solemn humiliation, with fastings,[27] and thanksgivings, upon special occasions, ought to be used in a holy and religious manner.[28]

6. Neither prayer nor any other part of religious worship, is now under the gospel, tied unto, or made more acceptable by any place in which it is performed, or towards which it is directed; but God is to be worshipped everywhere in spirit and in truth;[29] as in private families[30] daily,[31] and in secret each one by himself;[32] so more solemnly in the public assemblies, which are not carelessly nor willfully to be neglected or forsaken, when God by his word or providence calls thereunto.[33]

7. As it is the law of nature, that in general a proportion of time, by God's appointment, be set apart for the worship of God, so by his Word, in a positive moral, and perpetual commandment, binding all men, in all ages, he has particularly appointed one day in seven for a sabbath to be kept holy unto him,[34] which from the beginning of the world to the resurrection of Christ was the last day of the week, and from the resurrection of Christ was changed into the first day of the week, which is called the Lord's day:[35] and is to be continued to the end of the world as the Christian Sabbath, the observation of the last day of the week being abolished.

8. The sabbath is then kept holy unto the Lord, when men, after a due preparing of their hearts, and ordering their common affairs aforehand, do not only observe an holy rest all day, from their own works, words and thoughts, about their worldly employment and recreations,[36] but are also taken up the whole time in the public and private exercises of his worship, and in the duties of necessity and mercy.[37]

Answer

- What does the light of nature show?

- How should we respond to what the light of nature shows?

- Where do we find the acceptable way to worship God?

- Why must worship be regulated by this standard?

---

[27] Esther 4:16; Joel 2:12.
[28] Exodus 15:1-19, Psalm 107.
[29] Malachi 1:11; John 4:21; 1 Timothy 2:8.
[30] Acts 10:2.
[31] Psalm 55:17; Matthew 6:11.
[32] Matthew 6:6.
[33] Acts 2:42; Hebrews 10:25.
[34] Exodus 20:8.
[35] Acts 20:7; 1 Corinthians 16:1, 2; Revelation 1:10.
[36] Nehemiah 13:15-22; Isaiah 58:13.
[37] Matthew 12:1-13.

Confessing Sound Words

- Who is to be worshipped? Who is not to be worshipped?

- Who alone can serve as the mediator between God and man?

- What is required of all men? What makes it acceptable?

- Who is to be prayed for, and for who should prayers not be made?

- What are the good and acceptable elements/parts of religious worship?

- What is meant by "with understanding, faith, reverence, and godly fear?"

- What is to be done on special occasions?

- Under the gospel, where and how is worship to be rendered to God?

- What mustn't be neglected unless providentially hindered?

- Other than the public assembly, where is God to be worshipped?

- What is required by the law of nature?

- What day has God set apart for religious worship?

- How is the sabbath kept holy?

- What are some examples of works of necessity and works of mercy?

- What are some are the elements included in our church's corporate gatherings?

- What does family worship look like in your family?

- Why is keeping the Christian Sabbath difficult for many in our culture?

- What struggles have you had with keeping it?

- What can you do more consistently and faithfully keep the Christian Sabbath?

Chapter 23
Of Lawful Oaths and Vows

Part 1: Bible Study (Deuteronomy 10:12–21)
Read
- Read the passage multiple times.

- Read the passage in a few different translations.

- Take note of what is similar and what is different.

Context
- What type of literature is the passage? (Is it narrative, a gospel, prophecy, poetry, or something else?)

- What has happened so far in the story?

- What happened immediately before this passage? How do you think this passage and the one before it are connected?

- What comes immediately after this story?

Observation
- Who are the main characters in the story? What are we told about them?

- Where do the events in the story take place?

- Is there a problem in the story that needs resolution?

- What is the main point of the story or theme in the story?

- Is there anything that surprised or confused you?

Confessing Sound Words

Meaning
- Does the narrator of the story provide any commentary? If so, what does he say? How does this help give us clarity in what is being told us?

- Does anyone in the story learn something? Are they given a new command? If so, what did they learn? What were they commanded to do?

- Are there any threats made? What are they?

- Are there any promises made? What are they?

- Is this story taken up thematically, alluded to, or quoted elsewhere in the Bible? If so, what is said?

- How does this passage point to Jesus or find its ultimate fulfillment in him?

- Summarize the meaning or big idea(s) of this passage in your own words.

Application
- What does this passage call you to believe about God?

- What does this passage call you to do? What attitude or behaviour do you need to change?

- What does this passage teach us about vows and oaths?

Part 2: Scripture Memory (Deuteronomy 6:13)

Putting Deuteronomy 6:13 into context: Deuteronomy is the concluding book of the Pentateuch/Torah. It contains three addresses to the generation that would enter and take the land of Canaan. It includes a retelling of what had happened in the prior generation, a retelling of the Ten Commandments, instructions for life in the land, promises of blessing for obedience, and warnings of curses for disobedience. The prior generation with Moses would not enter the promised land due to their sin. This book is Moses' final words to His people.
- Read Deuteronomy 6:1–25.

- Who shall we fear?

- Who shall we serve?

- By who's name shall we swear?

- Why should we exercise care in swearing by God's name?

- What other things do people swear by?

- How do these violate the notion of lawful vows and oaths?

Part 3: Confession
Read

1. A lawful oath is a part of religious worship, wherein the person swearing in truth, righteousness, and judgement, solemnly calls God to witness what he swears,[1] and to judge him according to the truth or falseness thereof.[2]

2. The name of God only is that by which men ought to swear; and therein it is to be used, with all holy fear and reverence; therefore to swear vainly or rashly by that glorious and dreadful name, or to swear at all by any other thing, is sinful, and to be abhorred;[3] yet as in matter of weight and moment, for confirmation of truth, and ending all strife, an oath is warranted by the word of God;[4] so a lawful oath being imposed by lawful authority in such matters, ought to be taken.[5]

3. Whosoever takes an oath warranted by the Word of God, ought duly to consider the weightiness of so solemn an act, and therein to avouch[6] nothing but what he knows to be truth; for that by rash, false, and vain oaths, the Lord is provoked, and for them this land mourns.[7]

4. An oath is to be taken in the plain and common sense of the words, without equivocation or mental reservation (Psalm 24:4).

---

[1] Exodus 20:7; Deuteronomy 10:20; Jeremiah 4:2
[2] 2 Chronicles 6:22, 23
[3] Matthew 5:34, 37; James 5:12
[4] 2 Corinthians 1:23; Hebrews 6:16.
[5] Nehemiah 13:25.
[6] *Avouch* meaning to affirm.
[7] Leviticus 19:12; Jeremiah 23:10.

Confessing Sound Words

5. A vow, which is not to be made to any creature, but to God alone, is to be made and performed with all religious care and faithfulness;[8] but popish monastical vows of perpetual single life,[9] professed poverty,[10] and regular obedience, are so far from being degrees of higher perfection, that they are superstitious and sinful snares, in which no Christian may entangle himself.[11]

Answer

- How do we reconcile what the confession says about lawful oaths and vows with James 5:12 and 5:33–37?

- What is a lawful oath?

- By what only may men swear?

- What posture should men have when they make an oath?

- When is an oath lawful?

- To whom is an oath given?

- What should one consider when taking an oath?

- Summarize paragraph four in your own words?

- What is a vow?

- To whom is a vow made?

- How are vows to be performed?

- What are the differences and similarities between vows and oaths?

- Give some examples of vows or oaths you have given?

---

[8] Genesis 28:20–22; Psalm 76:11.
[9] 1 Corinthians 7:2, 9.
[10] Ephesians 4:28.
[11] Matthew 19:11.

Chapter 24
Of the Civil Magistrate

Part 1: Catechism (Q68–71)

Q68. What is the fifth commandment?

The fifth commandment is "Honour your father and your mother, that your days may be long in the land that the LORD your God is giving you."[1]

- Summarize this commandment in your own words.

Q69. What is required in the fifth commandment?

The fifth commandment requires preserving the honor and performing the duties belonging to everyone in their several places and relations as superiors, inferiors, or equals.[2]

- Read the Scripture references.

- How does the catechism expand the literal command to apply to a broader audience?

- What are some examples of the groups listed?

Q70. What is forbidden in the fifth commandment?

The fifth commandment forbids neglecting or transgressing the honour and duty which belong to everyone in their several places and relations.[3]

- Read the Scripture references.

- How would one neglect or transgress the honour and duty which belongs to the various groups mentioned in the previous question?

- How would this concept be applied in our relationship to the civil magistrate?

Q71. What is the reason attached to the fifth commandment?

---

[1] Exodus 20:12 ESV.
[2] Romans 12:10; Ephesians 5:21; 1 Peter 2:17.
[3] Ezekiel 34:2–4; Matthew 15:4–6; Romans 13:8.

Confessing Sound Words

The reason attached to the fifth commandment is a promise of long life and prosperity to all who keep this commandment—as far as it will serve for God's glory and their good.[4]

- Read the Scripture references.

- What do you make of this question and answer? Does this mean that there is a guarantee for long prosperous life for the one who obeys this command? Why or why not?

Part 2: Bible Study (Romans 13:1–7)

Read

- Read the passage multiple times.

- Read the passage in a few different translations.

- Take note of what is similar and what is different.

Context

- What sort of writing is this passage: a letter, narrative, poem, wisdom literature, and/or prophecy?

- Who wrote this book? How do you know?

- Who was he writing the letter to? What can you learn about them and the situation of the letter?

- What comes immediately before this passage? Are there any clues to the connection between the text under consideration and that which comes before it?

- What comes immediately after this passage? Are there any clues to the connection between the text under consideration and that which comes after it?

---

[4] Deuteronomy 5:16; Ephesians 6:2, 3.

Observation
- Are there any significant divisions or subpoints within the text?

- Are there any connecting words that help us trace the argument? (for, but, therefore, because)

- What is the main point or points?

- What surprises are there? What are some things you don't understand?

- What are the keywords? What words or ideas are repeated?

Meaning
- How does this passage relate to other parts later in the book?

- Does this passage say anything about Jesus? If so, what?

- What does this teach us about God?

- What does this passage say about us and our salvation?

- How could we sum up the meaning of this passage in our own words?

Application
- What are some differences between you and the original audience?

- How does this passage challenge or confirm your understanding?

- Does this passage and the truth within it call for a particular attitude or posture? If so, what? Is there some attitude you need to change?

- How does this passage call on you to live?

- What does this passage teach us about the civil magistrate?

Confessing Sound Words

Part 3: Scripture Memory (1 Peter 2:17; 1 Timothy 2:1–2)
Putting 1 Peter 2:17 into context: Peter writes this letter to a group of disoriented and discouraged group of Christians. They are these things because of the suffering they experience because of their faith. He charges them throughout the letter to be godly, imitating Christ and resting in His salvation. The memory verse is a summation of other commands dispersed in the letter.
- Read 1 Peter 2:13–3:22.

- Define the groups/beings listed in the memory verse.

- How are the commands in the memory verse expounded throughout 1 Peter 2:13–3:22?

- Define the various commands in the memory verse?

- What do we do if one of the groups/beings mentioned expects us to disobey another one?

Putting 1 Timothy 2:1, 2: This is the first of two letters written to Paul's faithful ministry companion and beloved son in the faith. A gifted young man, Timothy was given the task of leading the Ephesian church. This church needed a lot of careful reformation in doctrine and worship. Sprinkled throughout the book is the charge to be a godly example. One such sprinkle is found in the memory verse.
- Read 1 Timothy 2:1–15.

- Summarize the memory verses in your own words.

- What is the command of the memory verse?

- What are the reasons given for obeying the command?

- What are some practical ways to implement this command in your own life?

- What are some practical ways for your local church to obey this command?

Of the Civil Magistrate

Part 4: Confession

Read

1. God, the supreme Lord and King of all the world, has ordained civil magistrates to be under him, over the people, for his own glory and the public good; and to this end hath armed them with the power of the sword, for defense and encouragement of them that do good, and for the punishment of evil doers.[5]

2. It is lawful for Christians to accept and execute the office of a magistrate when called there unto; in the management whereof, as they ought especially to maintain justice and peace,[6] according to the wholesome laws of each kingdom and commonwealth, so for that end they may lawfully now, under the New Testament wage war upon just and necessary occasions.[7]

3. Civil magistrates being set up by God for the ends aforesaid; subjection, in all lawful things commanded by them, ought to be yielded by us in the Lord, not only for wrath, but for conscience sake;[8] and we ought to make supplications and prayers for kings and all that are in authority, that under them we may live a quiet and peaceable life, in all godliness and honesty.[9]

Answer

- What has God ordained?

- For what purpose and end has he ordained it?

- What is lawful for Christians?

- What must Christians especially do?

- What does the confession say of war?

- How should Christians relate to the civil magistrate? Why?

- What else should we do for those that govern us? Why?

- How do we apply the principles of this chapter to our relationship to our governmental systems?

---

[5] Romans 13:1-4.
[6] 2 Samuel 23:3; Psalm 82:3, 4.
[7] Luke 3:14.
[8] Romans 13:5-7; 1 Peter 2:17.
[9] 1 Timothy 2:1, 2.

Chapter 25
Of Marriage

Part 1: Bible Study (Matthew 19:1–12)

Read
- Read the passage multiple times.

- Read the passage in a few different translations.

- Take note of what is similar and what is different.

Context
- What sort of writing is this passage: a letter, narrative, poem, wisdom literature, and/or prophecy?

- What has happened so far? What notable characters have been introduced, and what notable events have taken place?

- What is before and after this passage?

- Are there any persons or places that are mentioned that you don't know? (Search them out earlier in the book or with a commentary)

Observation
- Who are the main characters? What do you learn about them?

- Is there any dialogue or speaking? Who speaks? What do they say?

- What is the main point or points?

- What surprises are there? What are some things you don't understand?

- What are the keywords? What words or ideas are repeated?

Confessing Sound Words

Meaning
- Does the author provide any commentary for the event? How does this help us understand the story?

- Is any behaviour commended or portrayed as positive? Is any behaviour rebuked or negatively portrayed?

- What does this passage teach us about Jesus (His Person and Work)?

- What does this teach us about God?

- How could we sum up the meaning of this passage in our own words?

Application
- What are some differences between you and the original audience?

- How does this passage challenge or confirm my understanding?

- Is there some attitude you need to change?

- What does this passage teach about being one of Jesus' disciples?

- What does this passage teach us about marriage?

Part 2: Scripture Memory (Mark 10:6–9)
Putting Mark 10:6–9 into context: Mark is a fast-moving theological biography of the Lord Jesus. In Mark 10:1–31, Jesus teaches his disciples how citizens of his kingdom are to live. In Mark 10:1–12 in particular, Jesus takes up the subject of divorce, which was originally raised by the Pharisees (10:1). Verses 6–9 provide us with God's view of marriage and divorce.
- Read Mark 10:1–12.

- Write out the memory verse in your own words.

- What verse do the Pharisees refer to in Mark 10:4?

- What does Jesus mean in 10:5?

- Where does Jesus go to refute the Pharisees and show God's design and end for marriage?

- What does this teach us about how to interpret the Bible?

- What does it mean that a husband and wife become one flesh?

- Over what relationship does the marriage relationship take priority?

- How does this passage speak to the issues of no-fault divorce, homosexuality, adultery, fornication, and transgenderism?

- What are some ways a church helps its members view marriage in the way that Jesus teaches?

Part 3: Confession
Read

1. Marriage is to be between one man and one woman; neither is it lawful for any man to have more than one wife, nor for any woman to have more than one husband at the same time.[1]

2. Marriage was ordained for the mutual help of husband and wife,[2] for the increase of mankind with a legitimate issue,[3][4] and the preventing of uncleanness.[5]

3. It is lawful for all sorts of people to marry, who are able with judgement to give their consent;[6] yet it is the duty of Christians to marry in the Lord;[7] and therefore such as profess the true religion, should not marry with infidels, or idolaters; neither should such as are godly, be unequally yoked, by marrying with such as are wicked in their life, or maintain damnable heresy.[8]

---

[1] Genesis 2:24; Malachi 2:15; Matthew 19:5, 6.
[2] Genesis 2:18.
[3] *Issue* meaning offspring.
[4] Genesis 1:28.
[5] 1 Corinthians 7:2, 9.
[6] 1 Timothy 4:3; Hebrews 13:4.
[7] 1 Corinthians 7:39.
[8] Nehemiah 13:25-27.

Confessing Sound Words

4. Marriage ought not to be within the degrees of consanguinity[9] or affinity,[10] forbidden in the Word;[11] nor can such incestuous marriages ever be made lawful, by any law of man or consent of parties, so as those persons may live together as man and wife.[12]

Answer

- Who is marriage to be between?

- What is explicitly not lawful according to the confession?

- What also is not lawful by necessary inference? Put differently, though not stated, what type of unions would the confession not consider lawful?

- For what was marriage ordained?

- For whom is it lawful to marry?

- What is required of the persons involved? Put differently what must they be able to do?

- What duty is required of the Christians for marriage?

- What is forbidden?

- What marriage unions does the Word forbid and nothing can undo?

- Read paragraphs five and six of the twenty-fourth chapter of the *Westminster Confession of Faith*.[13] You will notice these paragraphs are not in the *Second London Baptist Confession of Faith*. It is hard to know for certain why. That said, in what cases is divorce permissible according to the *Westminster Confession of Faith*?

---

[9] *Consanguinity* meaning being of the same blood or related.
[10] *Affinity* meaning related to a person by blood.
[11] Leviticus 18.
[12] Mark 6:18; 1 Corinthians 5:1.
[13] You can it side by side with the 2LBCF here: https://www.proginosko.com/docs/wcf_sdfo_lbcf.html#WCF29

- Why is it so important that we confess what the Bible teaches about marriage?

- What challenges are we facing today that make such confessing a challenge?

Chapter 26
Of the Church

Part 1: Catechism (Q101)

Q101. What is the duty of those rightly baptized?

It is the duty of those rightly baptized to become a member of a particular and orderly church of Jesus Christ, that they may walk blamelessly in all the commandments and ordinances of the Lord.[1]

- Read the Scripture references.

- Who has the duty to become "a member of a particular and orderly church?"

- Why should they join such a church?

- According to the Scripture references, what is an orderly church?

- Have you joined such a church? Why or why not?

- What could help a church be orderly?

- In what ways does being a church member "walk blamelessly in all commandments and ordinances of the Lord?"

Part 2: Bible Study (Matthew 18:15–20)

Read

- Read the passage multiple times.

- Read the passage in a few different translations.

- Take note of what is similar and what is different.

---

[1] Luke 1:6; Acts 2:41, 42; 5:13, 14; 9:26; 1 Peter 2:5.

Confessing Sound Words

Context
- What sort of writing is this passage: a letter, narrative, poem, wisdom literature, and/or prophecy?

- What has happened so far? What major characters have been introduced, and what significant events have taken place?

- What is before and after this passage?

- Are there any persons or places that are mentioned that you don't know? (Search them out earlier in the book, or with commentary)

Observation
- Who are the main characters? What do you learn about them?

- Is there any dialogue or speaking? Who speaks? What do they say?

- What is the main point or points?

- What surprises are there? What are some things you don't understand?

- What are the keywords? What words or ideas are repeated?

Meaning
- Does the author provide any commentary for the event? How does this help us understand the story?

- Is any behaviour commended or portrayed as positive? Is any behaviour rebuked or negatively portrayed?

- What does this passage teach us about Jesus (His Person and Work)?

- What does this teach us about God?

- How could we sum up the meaning of this passage in our own words?

Application
- What are some differences between you and the original audience?

- How does this passage challenge or confirm my understanding?

- Is there some attitude you need to change?

- What does this passage teach about being one of Jesus' disciples?

- What does this passage teach us about the church?

Part 3: Scripture Memory (Colossians 1:18; Acts 2:42; Hebrews 10:24, 25)
Putting Colossians 1:18 into context: In the letter of the Colossians is combatting some sort of gospel denying heresy. The heresy at its core denied the sufficiency of Christ's person and work for the salvation of sinners. The memory verse amid one of the most vivid and exalted portrayals of Christ Jesus (1:18-23).
- Read Colossians 1:15-23.

- What does this passage say about Jesus? (Look at the he/who is statements)

- What does our memory verse say about Jesus in particular?

- What does this teach us about the church? Thus, who orders and directs the church in its worship, polity, and mission?

Putting Acts 2:42 into context: Jesus had ascended and sent the Holy Spirit upon the apostles to empower them for their ministry, the establishing of the new covenant church. Our text comes at the end after Peter's sermon at Pentecost and the saving of thousands of souls and gives us insight into the workings of the early church.
- Read Acts 2:42-47.

- To what did the early church devote themselves? What do each of those terms mean?

- What would these elements look like in practice today?

Confessing Sound Words

Putting Hebrews 10:24, 25 into context: Like Colossians, the author of Hebrews calls his audience to cleave to the all-sufficient Christ. In particular, he encourages his suffering readers to not leave Jesus and return to the Old Testament ceremonial law.

- Read Hebrews 10:19–39.

- What actions are a part of the series of "let us" statements in verses 22 through 25?

- What is the ground or motivation for obeying these "let us" statements?

- What is the specific action called for in verses 24, 25?

- What is an act of disobedience to this "let us" statement?

- What is an act of obedience to it?

Part 4: Confession
Read

1. The catholic or universal church, which (with respect to the internal work of the Spirit and truth of grace) may be called invisible, consists of the whole number of the elect, that have been, are, or shall be gathered into one, under Christ, the head thereof; and is the spouse, the body, the fullness of him that fills all in all.[2]

2. All persons throughout the world, professing the faith of the gospel, and obedience unto God by Christ according unto it, not destroying their own profession by any errors everting the foundation, or unholiness of conversation,[3] are and may be called visible saints;[4] and of such ought all particular congregations to be constituted.[5]

3. The purest churches under heaven are subject to mixture and error;[6] and some have so degenerated as to become no churches of Christ, but synagogues of

---

[2] Ephesians 1:10, 22, 23; 5:23, 27, 32; Colossians 1:18; Hebrews 12:23.
[3] *Conversation* meaning the manner of conducting oneself in the world or in society.
[4] Acts 11:26; 1 Corinthians 1:2.
[5] Romans 1:7; Ephesians 1:20–22.
[6] Revelation 2; 3; 1 Corinthians 5.

Satan;⁷ nevertheless Christ always has had, and ever shall have a kingdom in this world, to the end thereof, of such as believe in him, and make profession of his name.⁸

4. The Lord Jesus Christ is the Head of the church, in whom, by the appointment of the Father, all power for the calling, institution, order or government of the church, is invested in a supreme and sovereign manner;⁹ neither can the Pope of Rome in any sense be head thereof, but is that antichrist, that man of sin, and son of perdition, that exalts himself in the church against Christ, and all that is called God; whom the Lord shall destroy with the brightness of his coming.¹⁰

5. In the execution of this power wherewith he is so entrusted, the Lord Jesus calls out of the world unto himself, through the ministry of his word, by his Spirit, those that are given unto him by his Father,¹¹ that they may walk before him in all the ways of obedience, which he prescribes to them in his word.¹² Those thus called, he commands to walk together in particular societies, or churches, for their mutual edification, and the due performance of that public worship, which he requires of them in the world.¹³

6. The members of these churches are saints by calling, visibly manifesting and evidencing (in and by their profession and walking) their obedience unto that call of Christ;¹⁴ and do willingly consent to walk together, according to the appointment of Christ; giving up themselves to the Lord, and one to another, by the will of God, in professed subjection to the ordinances of the Gospel.¹⁵

7. To each of these churches thus gathered, according to his mind declared in his word, he has given all that power and authority, which is in any way needful for their carrying on that order in worship and discipline, which he has instituted for them to observe; with commands and rules for the due and right exerting, and executing of that power.¹⁶

8. A particular church, gathered and completely organized according to the mind of Christ, consists of officers and members; and the officers appointed by Christ to be chosen and set apart by the church (so called and gathered), for the

---

⁷ 2 Thessalonians 2:11, 12; Revelation 18:2.
⁸ Psalm 72:17; 102:28; Matthew 16:18; Revelation 12:17.
⁹ Matthew 28:18-20; Ephesians 4:11, 12; Colossians 1:18.
¹⁰ 2 Thessalonians 2:2-9.
¹¹ John 10:16; 12:32.
¹² Matthew 28:20.
¹³ Matthew 18:15-20.
¹⁴ Romans 1:7; 1 Corinthians 1:2.
¹⁵ Acts 2:41, 42; 5:13, 14; 2 Corinthians 9:13.
¹⁶ Matthew 18:17, 18; 1 Corinthians 5:4, 5, 13; 2 Corinthians 2:6-8.

peculiar administration of ordinances, and execution of power or duty, which he entrusts them with, or calls them to, to be continued to the end of the world, are bishops or elders, and deacons.[17]

9. The way appointed by Christ for the calling of any person, fitted and gifted by the Holy Spirit, unto the office of bishop or elder in a church, is, that he be chosen thereunto by the common suffrage of the church itself;[18] and solemnly set apart by fasting and prayer, with imposition of hands of the eldership of the church, if there be any before constituted therein;[19] and of a deacon that he be chosen by the like suffrage, and set apart by prayer, and the like imposition of hands.[20]

10. The work of pastors being constantly to attend the service of Christ, in his churches, in the ministry of the word and prayer, with watching for their souls, as they that must give an account to Him;[21] it is incumbent on the churches to whom they minister, not only to give them all due respect, but also to communicate[22] to them of all their good things according to their ability,[23] so as they may have a comfortable supply, without being themselves entangled in secular affairs;[24] and may also be capable of exercising hospitality towards others;[25] and this is required by the law of nature, and by the express order of our Lord Jesus, who has ordained that they that preach the Gospel should live of the Gospel.[26]

11. Although it be incumbent on the bishops or pastors of the churches, to be instant in preaching the word, by way of office, yet the work of preaching the word is not so peculiarly confined to them but that others also gifted and fitted by the Holy Spirit for it, and approved and called by the church, may and ought to perform it.[27]

12. As all believers are bound to join themselves to particular churches, when and where they have opportunity so to do; so all that are admitted unto the privileges of a church, are also under the censures and government thereof, according to the rule of Christ.[28]

---

[17] Acts 20:17, 28; Philippians 1:1.
[18] Acts 14:23.
[19] 1 Timothy 4:14.
[20] Acts 6:3, 5, 6.
[21] Acts 6:4; Hebrews 13:17.
[22] *Communicate* meaning to give or offer something.
[23] Galatians 6:6, 7; 1 Timothy 5:17, 18.
[24] 2 Timothy 2:4.
[25] 1 Timothy 3:2.
[26] 1 Corinthians 9:6-14.
[27] Acts 11:19-21; 1 Peter 4:10, 11.
[28] 1 Thessalonians 5:14; 2 Thessalonians 3:6, 14, 15.

Of the Church

13. No church members, upon any offence taken by them, having performed their duty required of them towards the person they are offended at, ought to disturb any church-order, or absent themselves from the assemblies of the church, or administration of any ordinances, upon the account of such offence at any of their fellow members, but to wait upon Christ, in the further proceeding of the church.[29]

14. As each church, and all the members of it, are bound to pray continually for the good and prosperity of all the churches of Christ,[30] in all places, and upon all occasions to further it (every one within the bounds of their places and callings[31], in the exercise of their gifts and graces) so the churches (when planted by the providence of God so as they may enjoy opportunity and advantage for it) ought to hold communion[32] among themselves, for their peace, increase of love, and mutual edification.[33]

15. In cases of difficulties or differences, either in point of doctrine or administration, wherein either the churches in general are concerned, or any one church, in their peace, union, and edification; or any member or members of any church are injured, in or by any proceedings in censures not agreeable to truth and order: it is according to the mind of Christ, that many churches holding communion together, do, by their messengers, meet to consider, and give their advice in or about that matter in difference, to be reported to all the churches concerned;[34] howbeit[35] these messengers assembled, are not entrusted with any church-power properly so called; or with any jurisdiction over the churches themselves, to exercise any censures either over any churches or persons; or to impose their determination on the churches or officers.[36]

Answer

- Of whom is the catholic or universal church made up?

- Who are visible saints?

- Of whom should particular local churches be constituted?

---

[29] Matthew 18:15-17; Ephesians 4:2, 3.
[30] Psalm 122:6; Ephesians 6:18.
[31] *Places* and *callings* meaning a person's status, rank, or office. For example, a pastor holds an official position with specific responsibilities, qualifications, and gifts. A pastor could and should use his gift of teaching to bless the association of which his church is joined.
[32] *Communion* meaning formal membership or association.
[33] Romans 16:1, 2; 3 John 8-10.
[34] Acts 15:2, 4, 6, 22, 23, 25.
[35] *Howbeit* meaning nevertheless.
[36] 2 Corinthians 1:24; 1 John 4:1.

- To what are the purest churches under heaven subjected?

- What are those churches that have degenerated to the point of being not a church of Christ?

- What does Jesus always have in this world?

- Who is the head of the church? Who is not? What is the Pope of Rome identified as?

- What rights does Jesus have as head of the church?

- What does Jesus do with his power as head of the church?

- What are the means, and who is the agent by which he accomplishes these things?

- To whom does Jesus execute this power?

- What has Jesus commanded his elect to do? Why?

- Who are the members of these local and visible churches? What do they voluntarily do in joining or constituting a local church?

- What does each church have the power to do?

- What or who does a particular organized church consist of?

- What are some of the functions of these officers? How long are they to execute these functions?

- How are officers to be appointed and set apart?

- What is the work of pastors?

- What responsibilities does a church have to its pastor? What are the reasons given for these responsibilities?

Of the Church

- Who else may labour in the work of preaching the Word?

- Under what are all church members admitted to the privileges of a church?

- What shall members upon an offence against them do as it relates to the church and the process of discipline?

- When providence allows, what should all local churches do? Why?

- What are the functions of an association of local churches? What authority do associations have? What authority do they not have?

Chapter 27
Of the Communion of the Saints

Part 1: Bible Study (1 Corinthians 12:12–31)
Read
- Read the passage multiple times.

- Read the passage in a few different translations.

- Take note of what is similar and what is different.

Context
- What sort of writing is this passage: a letter, narrative, poem, wisdom literature, and/or prophecy?

- Who wrote this book? How do you know?

- Who was he writing the letter to? What can you learn about them and the situation of the letter?

- What comes immediately before this passage? Are there any clues to the connection between the text under consideration and that which comes before it?

- What comes immediately after this passage? Are there any clues to the connection between the text under consideration and that which comes after it?

Observation
- Are there any significant divisions or subpoints within the text?

- Are there any connecting words that help us trace the argument? (for, but, therefore, because)

- What is the main point or points?

- What surprises are there? What are some things you don't understand?

Confessing Sound Words

- What are the keywords? What words or ideas are repeated?

Meaning
- How does this passage relate to other parts later in the book?
- Does this passage say anything about Jesus? If so, what?
- What does this teach us about God?
- What does this passage say about us and our salvation?
- How could we sum up the meaning of this passage in our own words?

Application
- What are some differences between you and the original audience?
- How does this passage challenge or confirm your understanding?
- Does this passage and the truth within it call for a particular attitude or posture? If so, what? Is there some attitude you need to change?
- How does this passage call on you to live?
- What does this passage teach us about the communion of saints?

Part 2: Scripture Memory (1 John 1:2, 3; Galatians 6:2, 10)
Putting 1 John 1:2, 3 into context: 1 John is the first of three letters written by the apostle John. In this letter, he refutes false teachers and gives Christians different tests to check the legitimacy of our communion with God. In doing so, he drives us 1) analyze the fruit of teachers before we listen to them and 2) to Christ as the ground and rock of our assurance. The memory verses memorize the second point. The memory verses give rational for why John is writing.
- Read 1 John 1:1–4.
- What or who is the Word of life?

- Why does John proclaim it to his audience?

- With whom do believers have fellowship?

Putting Galatians 6:10 into context: Paul wrote this letter to a group of churches located near modern-day Turkey. He has proclaimed the gospel in these churches. This letter's purpose was to call them back to the gospel and refute the errors of those who would lead these churches away from it. There is only one gospel (Galatians 1:6–9), the gospel of free grace in Christ. Paul defends his apostolic authority in chapters one and two. He defends and explains the notion that all who place faith in Jesus partake of His salvation regardless of ethnicity in chapters 3 and 4. Chapters 5 and 6 show us that the gospel leads to freedom and godliness. Our memory verses emphasize the latter as it relates to other people, especially believers.

- Read Galatians 6:1–10.

- What does it mean to bear one another's burdens? What does it look like in our context?

- Though we are to do good to everyone, who is to be the believer's priority?

- What are some goods that we can do for others?

Part 3: Confession
Read

1. All saints that are united to Jesus Christ, their head, by his Spirit, and faith, although they are not made thereby one person with him, have fellowship in his graces, sufferings, death, resurrection, and glory;[1] and, being united to one another in love, they have communion in each other's gifts and graces,[2] and are obliged to the performance of such duties, public and private, in an orderly way, as do conduce to their mutual good, both in the inward and outward man.[3]

2. Saints by profession are bound to maintain a holy fellowship and communion in the worship of God, and in performing such other spiritual services as tend to

---

[1] John 1:16; Romans 6:5, 6; Philippians 3:10; 1 John 1:3.
[2] 1 Corinthians 3:21–23; 12:7; Ephesians 4:15, 16.
[3] Romans 1:12; Galatians 6:10; 1 Thessalonians 5:11, 14; 1 John 3:17, 18.

Confessing Sound Words

their mutual edification;[4] as also in relieving each other in outward things according to their several abilities, and necessities;[5] which communion, according to the rule of the gospel, though especially to be exercised by them, in the relation wherein they stand, whether in families,[6] or churches,[7] yet, as God offers opportunity, is to be extended to all the household of faith, even all those who in every place call upon the name of the Lord Jesus; nevertheless their communion one with another as saints, does not take away or infringe the title or propriety which each man has in his goods and possessions.[8]

Answer

- To whom are believers united first? To whom are believers united to second? (Our union with the first results in union with the second)

- What is not included in believers being united with Christ?

- What does Christ share with those who are united to him?

- What does our union with these two parties require as a proper response?

- What is the purpose of having communion with one another?

- What are saints by profession bound to maintain? Why?

- What else are they bound to maintain?

- Regarding the provision of needs what are the priorities the confession gives to professing saints? Over or to whom are saints to concern themselves first?

- When providence allows, whom else's needs are Christians to concern themselves?
- Does the confession's notion of communion with other saints erase or eliminate the notion of private property? Why or why not?

---

[4] Hebrews 3:12, 13; 10:24, 25.
[5] Acts 11:29, 30.
[6] Ephesians 6:4.
[7] 1 Corinthians 12:14–27.
[8] Acts 5:4; Ephesians 4:28.

Of the Communion of the Saints

- What are some ways you can commune with other saints?

- What reasons might someone give to not commune with other saints?

Chapter 28
Of Baptism and the Lord's Supper

Part 1: Catechism (Q93–96)

Q93. What are the outward means through by which Christ communicates the benefits of redemption to us?

The outward and ordinary means by which Christ communicates the benefits of redemption to us are His ordinances, especially the Word, baptism, the Lord's Supper, and prayer; all these means are made effectual to the elect for salvation.[1]

- Read all the Scripture references.

- What are the four ordinary means of grace listed?

- What does outward and ordinary mean in this context?

- What does it mean to say that these are ordinances?

- To whom are these made effectual for salvation?

Q94. How is the Word made effectual for salvation?

The Spirit of God makes the reading, but especially the preaching of the Word, an effectual means of convicting and converting sinners, and of building them up in holiness and comfort through faith unto salvation.[2]

- Read all the Scripture references.

- What person of the Godhead especially makes the ministry of the Word effectual for salvation?

- What are the different results the Spirit brings about through the ministry of the Word?

---

[1] Matthew 28:19, 20; Acts 2:42, 46, 47.
[2] Nehemiah 8:8; Psalm 19:8; Acts 20:32; 26:18; Romans 1:15, 16; 10:13–17; 15:4; 1 Corinthians 14:24, 25; 2 Timothy 3:15–17.

Confessing Sound Words

Q95. How is the Word to be read and heard, that it may become effectual for salvation?

That the Word may become effectual for salvation, we must attend to it with diligence, preparation, and prayer; receive it with faith and love, lay it up in our hearts, and practice it in our lives.[3]

- Read all the Scripture references.

- How must we attend to the Word?

- What does this look like in day to day life?

Q96. How do baptism and the Lord's Supper become effectual means of salvation?

Baptism and the Lord's Supper become effectual means of salvation, not for any virtue in them, or in him that does administer them, but only by the blessing of Christ, and the working of the Spirit in those that by faith receive them.[4]

- Read all the Scripture references.

- Who makes baptism and the Lord's Supper effectual means of salvation?

- How must they be received?

Part 2: Bible Study (2 Timothy 3:1–17)

Read

- Read the passage multiple times.

- Read the passage in a few different translations.

- Take note of what is similar and what is different.

---

[3] Psalm 119:11, 18; Proverbs 8:34; Luke 8:15; 2 Thessalonians 2:10; Hebrews 4:2; 1 Peter 2:1, 2; James 1:25.

[4] Matthew 3:11; 1 Corinthians 3:6, 7; 12:3; 1 Peter 3:21.

Of Baptism and the Lord's Supper

Context
- What sort of writing is this passage: a letter, narrative, poem, wisdom literature, and/or prophecy?

- Who wrote this book? How do you know?

- Who was he writing the letter to? What can you learn about them and the situation of the letter?

- What comes immediately before this passage? Are there any clues to the connection between the text under consideration and that which comes before it?

- What comes immediately after this passage? Are there any clues to the connection between the text under consideration and that which comes after it?

Observation
- Are there any significant divisions or subpoints within the text?

- Are there any connecting words that help us trace the argument? (for, but, therefore, because)

- What is the main point or points?

- What surprises are there? What are some things you don't understand?

- What are the keywords? What words or ideas are repeated?

Meaning
- How does this passage relate to other parts later in the book?

- Does this passage say anything about Jesus? If so, what?

- What does this teach us about God?

- What does this passage say about us and our salvation?

Confessing Sound Words

- How could we sum up the meaning of this passage in our own words?

Application
- What are some differences between you and the original audience?

- How does this passage challenge or confirm your understanding?

- Does this passage and the truth within it call for a particular attitude or posture? If so, what? Is there some attitude you need to change?

- How does this passage call on you to live?

- What does this passage teach us about the Word of God as an ordinary means of grace? Where should we expect to find the other ordinary means of grace?

Part 3: Scripture Memory (Matthew 28:18–20; 1 Corinthians 11:23)
Putting Matthew 28:18–20 into context: Before the memory verses, there is the report of Jesus' resurrection (Matthew 28:1–10). There is also the conspiring of the guards of the tomb and the religious leaders to spread the lie that Jesus' body was stolen by the disciples while the guards were asleep (28:11–15). The eleven disciples went to where Jesus had directed them in Galilee, and Jesus comes to meet them. Some worship, and some doubted. In the memory verses, there are words of comfort and a charge.
- Read Matthew 28:16–20.

- What is the first word of comfort Jesus gives? What truth does he declare about himself?

- What command does Jesus give his apostles and the church for which they serve as the foundation?

- How do they carry out this command?

- What is the second word of comfort Jesus gives?

Of Baptism and the Lord's Supper

- What does this passage teach us about baptism?

Putting 1 Corinthians 11:26 into context: 1 Corinthians is written to the church in Corinth, one of the trading centers in the ancient world. The church was burdened by many problems, including sexual immorality and division. The division within the church affected how they administered the Lord's Supper (11:17–34). Some gorged themselves while others did not eat. Some got drunk while others did not drink. The passage comes amid Paul's summary and correction of the problems.

- Read 1 Corinthians 11:17–34.

- Look at verse 23. Who gave this ordinance to Paul?

- Why is it so serious to take of the Lord's Supper in a divided and disorderly manner?

- Where and among whom is the Lord's Supper to be taken?

- What does the Lord's Supper proclaim?

Part 4: Confession
Read

1. Baptism and the Lord's Supper are ordinances of positive and sovereign institution,[5] appointed by the Lord Jesus, the only lawgiver, to be continued in his church to the end of the world.[6]

2. These holy appointments are to be administered by those only who are qualified and thereunto called, according to the commission of Christ.[7]

Answer

- What are the two ordinances? Who appointed them?

- How are they given? What does this mean?

---

[5] *Positive and sovereign institution* meaning these ordinances are not according to the law of nature but attached to a specific covenant for the present age. They are sovereignly given by Christ the mediator of the New Covenant. See footnote 35 of chapter two.
[6] Matthew 28:19, 20; 1 Corinthians 11:26.
[7] Matthew 28:19; 1 Corinthians 4:1.

Confessing Sound Words

- How long is their duration?

- Who is to administer them? According to whom?

Chapter 29
Of Baptism[1]

Part 1: Catechism (Q97–100)

Q97. What is baptism?

Baptism is an ordinance of the New Testament instituted by Jesus Christ. To the party baptized, it is a sign of fellowship with Him in His death, burial, and resurrection. Moreover, it is a sign of his being engrafted into Him, the remission of sins, and his giving up himself to God through Jesus Christ to live and walk in newness of life.[2]

- Read the Scripture references.

- Who instituted baptism as an ordinance?

- Of what is a baptism a sign?

- Have you been baptized? If so, then consider your baptism. How did it point things which it is said here to signify? If not, consider baptisms you have seen and answer the same question.

- To whom is it a sign?

- If you have been baptized, do you ever reflect on it and the truths of which it signifies? If so, what are your common takeaways from such reflection? If not, what keeps you from doing this?

Q98. To whom is baptism to be administered?

Baptism is to be administered to all those who actually profess repentance toward God, faith in, and obedience to our Lord Jesus Christ, and to no other.[3]

- Read the Scripture references.

- What must one do before they receive Christian baptism?

---

[1] See the appendix on Baptism for fuller explanation on why the framers of this confession rejected infant baptism.
[2] Matthew 28:19; Mark 1:4; Acts 2:38; 22:16; Romans 6:3-5; Galatians 3:27; Colossians 2:12.
[3] Matthew 3:6; 28:19; Mark 16:16; Acts 2:37, 38; 8:36-38.

Confessing Sound Words

- Should anyone who has not done these things be baptized? Why or why not?

Q99. Are infants of professing believers to be baptized?
The infants of professing believers are not to be baptized because there is neither command nor example in the Holy Scriptures or certain consequence from them to baptize such.[4]

- Read the Scripture references.

- Who should not be baptized?

- Why should they not be baptized?

Q100. How is Baptism rightly administered?
Baptism is rightly administered by immersion, or dipping the whole body of the party in water, into the name of the Father, and of the Son, and of the Holy Spirit, according to Christ's institution, and the practice of the apostles, and not by sprinkling or pouring of water, or dipping some part of the body, after the tradition of men.[5]

- Read the Scripture references.

- What is the proper mode of baptism?

- In whose name is someone to be baptized?

- What are improper modes of baptism?

Part 2: Bible Study (Acts 2:14–38)
Read
- Read the passage multiple times.

- Read the passage in a few different translations.

- Take note of what is similar and what is different.

---

[4] Proverbs 30:5; Luke 3:7, 8.
[5] Matthew 3:16; 28:19, 20; John 3:23; Acts 3:38; 10:48; Romans 6:4; Colossians 2:12.

Context
- What sort of writing is this passage: a letter, narrative, poem, wisdom literature, and/or prophecy?

- What has happened so far? What major characters have been introduced, and what significant events have taken place?

- What is before and after this passage?

- Are there any persons or places that are mentioned that you don't know? (Search them out earlier in the book or with a commentary)

Observation
- Who are the main characters? What do you learn about them?

- Is there any dialogue or speaking? Who speaks? What do they say?

- What is the main point or points?

- What surprises are there? What are some things you don't understand?

- What are the keywords? What words or ideas are repeated?

Meaning
- Does the author provide any commentary for the event? How does this help us understand the story?

- Is any behaviour commended or portrayed as positive? Is any behaviour rebuked or negatively portrayed?

- What does this passage teach us about Jesus (His Person and Work)?

- What does this teach us about God?

- How could we sum up the meaning of this passage in our own words?

Confessing Sound Words

Application
- What are some differences between you and the original audience?

- How does this passage challenge or confirm your understanding?

- Is there some attitude you need to change?

- What does this passage teach about being one of Jesus' disciples?

- What does this passage teach us about the ordinance of baptism?

Part 3: Scripture Memory (Acts 8:36, 38; Romans 6:3, 4)
Putting Acts 8:36, 38 into context: The gospel of the Lord Jesus had been preached in Jerusalem and Judea. It was beginning to be preached in Samaria. In our memory verse, we begin to see that it was being preached to those who lived in that region within the ends of the earth (Acts 1:8). Our text deals with a providential encounter, a reading and exposition of Scripture, and a soul added to the church. Upon His believing on the Lord Jesus Christ, the man is baptized at the nearest place in which the ordinance could be completed.
- Read Acts 8:26–40.

- What is the relationship between faith and baptism?

- What is needed for a baptism to be performed?

- Who by implication are the proper subjects for baptism?

Putting Romans 6:3, 4 into context: Romans is the longest letter of the apostle Paul. Romans 1:16–17 teaches revelation of God's righteousness in the Gospel. Romans 1:18–3:20 teaches the universal unrighteousness of humanity. Romans 3:21–5:21 teaches God's righteousness in justifying sinners in Christ by faith. Romans 6–8 teaches how the grace that justifies also reigns over the lives of those it justifies in Christ. (I suggest that you review your Bible Study from chapter 13).
- Read Romans 6:1–14.

- Into what have believers been baptized?

Of Baptism

- How does our union with Christ pictured in baptism inform or transform how we live?

Part 4: Confession

Read

1. Baptism is an ordinance of the New Testament, ordained by Jesus Christ, to be unto the party baptized, a sign of his fellowship with him, in his death and resurrection; of his being engrafted into him;[6] of remission of sins;[7] and of giving up into God, through Jesus Christ, to live and walk in newness of life.[8]

2. Those who do actually profess repentance towards God, faith in, and obedience to, our Lord Jesus Christ, are the only proper subjects of this ordinance.[9]

3. The outward element to be used in this ordinance is water, wherein the party is to be baptized, in the name of the Father, and of the Son, and of the Holy Spirit.[10]

4. Immersion, or dipping of the person in water, is necessary to the due administration of this ordinance.[11]

Answer

- Where is baptism ordained, and who ordained it?

- Of what is baptism a sign?

- How does it signify these things?

- Who are the proper subjects of baptism?

- What is the outward element to be used in this ordinance?

- What is the proper mode of baptism? Why?

---

[6] Romans 6:3–5; Galatians 3:27; Colossians 2:12.
[7] Mark 1:4; Acts 22:16.
[8] Romans 6:2, 4.
[9] Mark 16:16; Acts 2:41; 8:12, 36, 37; 18:8.
[10] Matthew 28:19, 20; Acts 8:38.
[11] Matthew 3:16; John 3:23.

Chapter 30
Of the Lord's Supper

Part 1: Catechism (Q102–104)

Q102. What is the Lord's Supper?

The Lord's Supper is an ordinance of the New Testament instituted by Jesus Christ. By giving and receiving bread and wine according to His appointment, His death is shown forth. Worthy receivers are not physically but spiritually by faith made partakers of Christ's body and blood with all His benefits. The result is their spiritual nourishment and growth in grace.[1]

- Read all the Scripture references.

- Who instituted the Lord's Supper?

- What are the elements of the Lord's Supper? What is given and received?

- What is shown forth by giving and receiving the elements?

- In what manner do we partake of Christ's body and blood?

- What is the result?

Q103. Who are the proper subjects of this ordinance?

The proper subjects of this ordinance are those who have been baptized upon a profession of their faith in Jesus Christ and repentance from dead works.[2]

- Read all the Scripture references.

- What is required to be a proper subject of the Lord's Supper?

---

[1] Matthew 26:26–28; 1 Corinthians 11:23–26; 10:16.
[2] Acts 2:41, 42.

Confessing Sound Words

Q104. What is required to receive the Lord's Supper worthily?

It is required of those who desire to worthily partake of the Lord's Supper that they examine themselves. They must examine their knowledge to discern the Lord's body, their faith to feed upon Him, their repentance, love, and new obedience; lest coming unworthily, they eat and drink judgement to themselves.[3]

- Read all the Scripture references.

- What must those who desire to worthily partake of the Lord's Supper do?

- What must be examined?

- What are the dangers of receiving the Lord's Supper unworthily?

Part 2: Bible Study (1 Corinthians 11:17–33)
Read
- Read the passage multiple times.

- Read the passage in a few different translations.

- Take note of what is similar and what is different.

Context
- What sort of writing is this passage: a letter, narrative, poem, wisdom literature, and/or prophecy?

- Who wrote this book? How do you know?

- Who was he writing the letter to? What can you learn about them and the situation of the letter?

- What comes immediately before this passage? Are there any clues to the connection between the text under consideration and that which comes before it?

---

[3] 1 Corinthians 5:7, 8; 10:16, 17; 11:28, 29, 31; 2 Corinthians 13:5.

- What comes immediately after this passage? Are there any clues to the connection between the text under consideration and that which comes after it?

Observation
- Are there any significant divisions or subpoints within the text?
- Are there any connecting words that help us trace the argument? (for, but, therefore, because)
- What is the main point or points?
- What surprises are there? What are some things you don't understand?
- What are the keywords? What words or ideas are repeated?

Meaning
- How does this passage relate to other parts later in the book?
- Does this passage say anything about Jesus? If so, what?
- What does this teach us about God?
- What does this passage say about us and our salvation?
- How could we sum up the meaning of this passage in our own words?

Application
- What are some differences between you and the original audience?
- How does this passage challenge or confirm your understanding?
- Does this passage and the truth within it call for a particular attitude or posture? If so, what? Is there some attitude you need to change?
- How does this passage call on you to live?

Confessing Sound Words

- What does this passage teach us about the Lord's Supper?

Part 3: Scripture Memory (1 Corinthians 10:16, 17; 1 Corinthians 11:28, 29)
Putting 1 Corinthians 10:16, 17 into context: 1 Corinthians is written to the church in Corinth, one of the trading centers in the ancient world. The church was encumbered by many problems, including sexual immorality and division. Our passage comes amid Paul's warning against idolatry. To partake of the sacrifices made to idols is to spiritually dine with and upon demons, who stand behind the idols. To partake of the Lord's Supper is to spiritually dine with and upon Christ.

- Read 1 Corinthians 10:1–22.

- What is the answer to the two questions in verse 16?

- In what do those who partake of the cup and the bread participate?

- What does this participation mean?

- How is the Lord's Supper to be taken (divided or united)?

- How does this passage confirm that the Lord's Supper is more than a mere memory but a means of grace?

Putting 1 Corinthians 11:28, 29 into context: The divisions within the church in Corinth affected how they administered the Lord's Supper (11:17–34). Some gorged themselves while others did not eat. Some got drunk while others did not drink. Our passage comes amid Paul's summary and correction of the problems.

- Review your Bible study in part 2 and reread 1 Corinthians 11:17–33.

- What should everyone do before partaking of the Lord's Supper?

- Why should everyone do this thing?

Part 4: Confession
Read

1. The supper of the Lord Jesus was instituted by him the same night wherein he was betrayed, to be observed in his churches, unto the end of the world, for the perpetual remembrance, and showing to all the world the sacrifice of himself in his death,[4] confirmation of the faith of believers in all the benefits thereof, their spiritual nourishment, and growth in him, their further engagement in, and to all duties which they owe to him; and to be a bond and pledge of their communion with him, and with each other.[5]

2. In this ordinance Christ is not offered up to his Father, nor any real sacrifice made at all for remission of sin of the quick or dead, but only a memorial of that one offering up of himself by himself upon the cross, once for all;[6] and a spiritual oblation[7] of all possible praise unto God for the same.[8] So that the popish sacrifice of the mass, as they call it, is most abominable, injurious to Christ's own sacrifice the alone propitiation for all the sins of the elect.

3. The Lord Jesus has, in this ordinance, appointed his ministers to pray, and bless the elements of bread and wine, and thereby to set them apart from a common to a holy use, and to take and break the bread; to take the cup, and, they communicating also themselves, to give both to the communicants.[9]

4. The denial of the cup to the people, worshipping the elements, the lifting them up, or carrying them about for adoration, and reserving them for any pretended[10] religious use, are all contrary to the nature of this ordinance, and to the institution of Christ.[11]

5. The outward elements in this ordinance, duly set apart to the use ordained by Christ, have such relation to him crucified, as that truly, although in terms used figuratively, they are sometimes called by the names of the things they represent, to wit,[12] the body and blood of Christ,[13] albeit, in substance and nature, they still remain truly and only bread and wine, as they were before.[14]

---

[4] 1 Corinthians 11:23–26.
[5] 1 Corinthians 10:16, 17, 21.
[6] Hebrews 9:25, 26, 28.
[7] *Oblation* meaning gift or offering.
[8] Matthew 26:26, 27; 1 Corinthians 11:24.
[9] 1 Corinthians 11:23–26.
[10] *Pretended* meaning counterfeit or feigned.
[11] Exodus 20:4, 5; Matthew 15:9; 26:26–28.
[12] *To wit* meaning namely.
[13] 1 Corinthians 11:27.
[14] 1 Corinthians 11:26–28.

6. That doctrine which maintains a change of the substance of bread and wine, into the substance of Christ's body and blood, commonly called transubstantiation, by consecration of a priest, or by any other way, is repugnant not to Scripture alone,[15] but even to common sense and reason, overthrows the nature of the ordinance, and has been, and is, the cause of manifold superstitions, yea, of gross idolatries.[16]

7. Worthy receivers, outwardly partaking of the visible elements in this ordinance, do then also inwardly by faith, really and indeed, yet not carnally and corporally, but spiritually receive, and feed upon Christ crucified, and all the benefits of his death; the body and blood of Christ being then not corporally or carnally,[17] but spiritually present to the faith of believers in that ordinance, as the elements themselves are to their outward senses.[18]

8. All ignorant and ungodly persons, as they are unfit to enjoy communion with Christ, so are they unworthy of the Lord's table, and cannot, without great sin against him, while they remain such, partake of these holy mysteries, or be admitted thereunto;[19] yea, whosoever shall receive unworthily, are guilty of the body and blood of the Lord, eating and drinking judgement to themselves.[20]

Answer

- Who instituted the Lord's Supper and when did he do it?

- Where is the Lord's Supper to be observed and how long?

- What are the results of observing the Lord's Supper?

- What does not happen during the observation of this ordinance? What does happen? What does this mean for the Catholic practice of the Lord's Supper?

- Who is to bless the elements and preside over the Lord's Supper? Who is to receive both the cup and the bread?

---

[15] Luke 24:6, 39; Acts 3:21.
[16] 1 Corinthians 11:24, 25.
[17] *Carnally* and *corporally* meaning bodily or physically.
[18] 1 Corinthians 10:16; 11:23–26.
[19] 2 Corinthians 6:14, 15.
[20] Matthew 7:6; 1 Corinthians 11:29.

Of the Lord's Supper

- What practices are contrary to the nature of this ordinance and Christ's institution?

- Are these elements sometimes called by that which they signify? Is this a figurative or literal use of these words?
- What overthrows the notions of the doctrine of transubstantiation?

- In what manner do worthy receivers of the Supper partake of Christ's body and blood? In what manner is Jesus present?

- Who is unworthy of the ordinance? Of what are those who partake of the Supper in an unworthy manner guilty?

Chapter 31
Of the State of Man after Death
and Of the Resurrection of the Dead

Part 1: Catechism (Q40–43)

Q40. What benefits do believers receive from Christ at their death?

At their death, the souls of believers are made perfect in holiness and immediately pass into glory. Their bodies, being still united to Christ, do rest in their graves until the resurrection.[1]

- Read all the Scripture references.

- What happens to the soul of believers at their death?

- What happens to the body, and for how long?

Q41. What benefits do believers receive from Christ at the resurrection?

At the resurrection, believers, being raised up in glory, will be openly acknowledged, acquitted in the Day of Judgement, and made perfectly blessed, in both soul and body, in full enjoyment of God to all eternity.[2]

- Read all the Scripture references.

- How will they be acknowledged at the resurrection?

- What will happen to them on the day of judgement?

- What comfort is gained in knowing that when Christ returns, we will have full enjoyment of God?

---

[1] Job 19:26, 27; Isaiah 57:2; Luke 23:43; 2 Corinthians 5:1, 6, 8; Philippians 1:23; 1 Thessalonians 4:14; Hebrews 12:23.
[2] Matthew 10:32; 25:23; 1 Corinthians 13:12; 15:43; 1 Thessalonians 4:17, 18; 1 John 3:2.

Confessing Sound Words

Q42. What will be done to the wicked at their death?
At their death, the souls of the wicked will be cast into the torments of hell, and their bodies will lie in their graves until the resurrection and judgement of the great day.[3]

- Read all the Scripture references.

- Where do the souls of the wicked go?

- What happens to their bodies?

- How long will they remain in this state?

Q43. What will be done to the wicked on the day of judgement?
On the day of judgement, the bodies of the wicked, being raised out of their graves, will be sentenced together with their souls to unspeakable torments with the devil and his angels forever.[4]

- Read all the Scripture references.

- Will the wicked also be raised? When?

- How long will their torments last?

Part 2: Bible Study (1 Corinthians 15:12–28)
Read

- Read the passage multiple times.

- Read the passage in a few different translations.

- Take note of what is similar and what is different.

---

[3] Psalm 49:14; Luke 16:23, 24; Acts 1:25; 1 Peter 3:19; Jude 7.
[4] Matthew 25:41, 46; John 5:28, 29; 2 Thessalonians 1:8, 9.

Of the State of Man after Death and Of the Resurrection of the Dead

Context
- What sort of writing is this passage: a letter, narrative, poem, wisdom literature, and/or prophecy?

- Who wrote this book? How do you know?

- Who was he writing the letter to? What can you learn about them and the situation of the letter?

- What comes immediately before this passage? Are there any clues to the connection between the text under consideration and that which comes before it?

- What comes immediately after this passage? Are there any clues to the connection between the text under consideration and that which comes after it?

Observation
- Are there any significant divisions or subpoints within the text?

- Are there any connecting words that help us trace the argument? (for, but, therefore, because)

- What is the main point or points?

- What surprises are there? What are some things you don't understand?

- What are the keywords? What words or ideas are repeated?

Meaning
- How does this passage relate to other parts later in the book?

- Does this passage say anything about Jesus? If so, what?

- What does this teach us about God?

- What does this passage say about us and our salvation?

- How could we sum up the meaning of this passage in our own words?

Confessing Sound Words

Application
- What are some differences between you and the original audience?

- How does this passage challenge or confirm your understanding?

- Does this passage and the truth within it call for a particular attitude or posture? If so, what? Is there some attitude you need to change?

- How does this passage call on you to live?

- What does this passage teach us about the state of man after death and the resurrection of the dead?

Part 3: Scripture Memory (Luke 23:43; Luke 16:22, 23; 1 Corinthians 15:51, 52; John 5:28, 29)
Putting Luke 23:43 into context: The memory verse comes amid the crucifixion of Christ. He has been placed between two criminals. One mocked the Lord, and the second rebuked the first. He acknowledges the justice of his own demise and the injustice of Jesus' death. Jesus' words in our verse are a response to the man's plea.
- Read Luke 23:26–43.

- Where would this man be, and who would he be with when he died?

Putting Luke 16:22, 23 into context: The memory verses come in the middle of one of Jesus' parables. In the parable, Jesus shows the destinations of the wicked and saints. He also shows a glimpse of the hardness of the human heart. The verse, in particular, deals with what is commonly referred to as the intermediate state.
- Read Luke 16:19–31.

- How is the intermediate state illustrated in this parable?

- How does the place in which the rich man went contrast with the place Lazarus went?

Of the State of Man after Death and Of the Resurrection of the Dead

Putting 1 Corinthians 15:51, 52 into context: 1 Corinthians is written to the church in Corinth, one of the trading centers in the ancient world. The church was encumbered by many problems, including sexual immorality and division. The passage comes amid Paul's discussion of Jesus' resurrection and the resurrection of his people.

- Read 1 Corinthians 15:50–58.

- What is the mystery Paul shares?

- What will not happen to some?

- What will happen to all?

- When will these things happen?

Putting John 5:28, 29 into context: In the passage the memory verse comes from, Jesus describes the nature of his authority as the Son of God. He has life in himself as the Father does. He gives life as the Father does. To dishonour him is to dishonour the Father, for they are the same in essence. That said, the verses focus on the final resurrection from the dead of all people.

- Read John 5:19–29.

- What will be heard at the coming hour?

- Who will hear it?

- What will happen to those who hear: doers of good and doers of evil?

Part 4: Confession
Read

1. The bodies of men after death return to dust, and see corruption;[5] but their souls, which neither die nor sleep, having an immortal subsistence,[6] immediately

---

[5] Genesis 3:19; Acts 13:36.
[6] *Subsistence* meaning existence or being.

Confessing Sound Words

return to God who gave them.⁷ The souls of the righteous being then made perfect in holiness, are received into paradise, where they are with Christ, and behold the face of God in light and glory, waiting for the full redemption of their bodies;⁸ and the souls of the wicked are cast into hell; where they remain in torment and utter darkness, reserved to the judgement of the great day;⁹ besides these two places, for souls separated from their bodies, the Scripture acknowledges none.

2. At the last day, such of the saints as are found alive, shall not sleep, but be changed;¹⁰ and all the dead shall be raised up with the selfsame¹¹ bodies, and none other;¹² although with different qualities, which shall be united again to their souls forever.¹³

3. The bodies of the unjust shall, by the power of Christ, be raised to dishonour; the bodies of the just, by his Spirit, unto honour, and be made conformable to his own glorious body.¹⁴

Answer

- What happens to the bodies of those who die?

- What happens to their souls? What does not happen to their souls? Why?

- What is the destination of the souls of the righteous?

- With whom are they?

- What do they behold?

- For what do they wait?

- What is the destination of the souls of the wicked?

- How many places are there where the souls of men go after death?

---

[7] Ecclesiastes 12:7.
[8] Luke 23:43; 2 Corinthians 5:1, 6, 8; Philippians 1:23; Hebrews 12:23.
[9] Luke 16:23, 24; 1 Peter 3:19; Jude 6, 7.
[10] 1 Corinthians 15:51, 52; 1 Thessalonians 4:17.
[11] *Selfsame* meaning exactly the same or the identical.
[12] Job 19:26, 27.
[13] 1 Corinthians 15:42, 43.
[14] John 5:28, 29; Acts 24:15; Philippians 3:21.

Of the State of Man after Death and Of the Resurrection of the Dead

- What will happen to the bodies of the saints on the last day?

- What will happen to the bodies of the unjust?

- How might the truths of this chapter motivate us to be more diligent and bolder in evangelism?

- How do the truths of this chapter provide us encouragement when facing suffering and death?

Chapter 32
Of the Last Judgement

Part 1: Bible Study (Matthew 25:31–46)
Read
- Read the passage multiple times.
- Read the passage in a few different translations.
- Take note of what is similar and what is different.

Context
- What sort of writing is this passage: a letter, narrative, poem, wisdom literature, and/or prophecy?
- What has happened so far? What major characters have been introduced, and what significant events have taken place?
- What is before and after this passage?
- Are there any persons or places that are mentioned that you don't know? (Search them out earlier in the book or with a commentary)

Observation
- Who are the main characters? What do you learn about them?
- Is there any dialogue or speaking? Who speaks? What do they say?
- What is the main point or points?
- What surprises are there? What are some things you don't understand?
- What are the keywords? What words or ideas are repeated?

Confessing Sound Words

Meaning
- Does the author provide any commentary for the event? How does this help us understand the story?

- Is any behaviour commended or portrayed as positive? Is any behaviour rebuked or negatively portrayed?

- What does this passage teach us about Jesus (His Person and Work)?

- What does this teach us about God?

- How could we sum up the meaning of this passage in our own words?

Application
- What are some differences between you and the original audience?

- How does this passage challenge or confirm your understanding?

- Is there some attitude you need to change?

- What does this passage teach about being one of Jesus' disciples?

- What does this passage teach us about the last judgement?

Part 2: Scripture Memory (2 Corinthians 5:10; Revelation 22:20)
Putting 2 Corinthians 5:10 into context: The memory verse is in the middle of the last letter Paul sent to the Corinthians. In the first letter, Paul called the Corinthian church to unity within. The second one called them to unity with him. The memory verse comes at the end of Paul's explanation why he and his ministry companions are "of good courage" in the face of suffering.
- Read 2 Corinthians 5:1–10.

- Why should we make it our aim to please Christ?

- How are the resurrection and the last judgement motivations for faithfulness to Christ?

Of the Last Judgement

- Before whom will we all appear?

- What will we receive on that day?

Putting Revelation 22:20 into context: The memory verse comes at the end of John's revelation. This revelation is recorded and sent to bless its readers who are in the tribulation (Revelation 1:3, 9). Instruction has been given to churches. Redemptive history has been retold in symbolic and apocalyptic language. The victory of Jesus over all his enemies and the salvation of his people is certain. Jesus will return to finish what was inaugurated in his first coming. The verse is a quotation followed by a prayer.

- Read Revelation 22:6–21.

- Who testifies these things?

- What are these things?

- What does the one who testifies say?

- What does John pray?

Part 3: Confession
Read

1. God has appointed a day wherein he will judge the world in righteousness, by Jesus Christ;[1] to whom all power and judgement is given of the Father; in which day, not only the apostate angels shall be judged,[2] but likewise all persons that have lived upon the earth shall appear before the tribunal of Christ, to give an account of their thoughts, words, and deeds, and to receive according to what they have done in the body, whether good or evil.[3]

2. The end of God's appointing this day, is for the manifestation of the glory of his mercy, in the eternal salvation of the elect; and of his justice, in the eternal

---

[1] John 5:22, 27; Acts 17:31.
[2] 1 Corinthians 6:3; Jude 6.
[3] Ecclesiastes 12:14; Matthew 12:36; 25:32–46; Romans 14:10, 12; 2 Corinthians 5:10.

damnation of the reprobate, who are wicked and disobedient;[4] for then shall the righteous go into everlasting life, and receive that fullness of joy and glory with everlasting rewards, in the presence of the Lord; but the wicked, who know not God, and obey not the gospel of Jesus Christ, shall be cast aside into everlasting torments,[5] and punished with everlasting destruction, from the presence of the Lord, and from the glory of his power.[6]

3. As Christ would have us to be certainly persuaded that there shall be a day of judgement, both to deter all men from sin,[7] and for the greater consolation of the godly in their adversity,[8] so will he have the day unknown to men, that they may shake off all carnal security, and be always watchful, because they know not at what hour the Lord will come,[9] and may ever be prepared to say, Come Lord Jesus; come quickly.[10] Amen.

Answer

- What has God appointed?

- By whom will he do this act?

- What has the Father given Christ?

- Who will appear before Jesus' tribunal?

- Of what will everyone give an account?

- What is God's end for appointing this day?

- How will the glory of God's mercy be shown?

- How will the glory of God's justice be shown?

- Where shall the righteous go after the judgement?

---

[4] Romans 9:22, 23.
[5] Matthew 25:21, 34; 2 Timothy 4:8.
[6] Matthew 25:46; Mark 9:48; 2 Thessalonians 1:7-10.
[7] 2 Corinthians 5:10, 11.
[8] 2 Thessalonians 1:5-7.
[9] Mark 13:35-37; Luke 12:35-40.
[10] Revelation 22:20.

- Where shall the wicked go after the judgement?

- Why would Christ have us be certain of such a day?

- Why will the day remain unknown until its arrival?

- What shall we all be ready to say?

Ending Statement, Signatories, and Appendix on Baptism

Ending Statement

We the ministers, and messengers of, and concerned for upwards of, one hundred baptized churches, in England and Wales (denying Arminianisim)[1], being met together in London, from the third of the seventh month to the eleventh of the same, 1689, to consider of some things that might be for the glory of God, and the good of these congregations, have thought meet[2] (for the satisfaction of all other Christians that differ from us in the point of Baptism) to recommend to their perusal the confession of our faith, which confession we own, as containing the doctrine of our faith and practice, and do desire that the members of our churches respectively do furnish themselves therewith.

Signatories

Hansard Knollys, Pastor, Broken Wharf, London
William Kiffin, Pastor, Devonshire-square, London
John Harris, Pastor, Joiner's Hall, London
William Collins, Pastor, Petty France, London
Hercules Collins, Pastor, Wapping, London
Robert Steed, Pastor, Broken Wharf, London
Leonard Harrison, Pastor, Limehouse, London
George Barret, Pastor, Mile End Green, London
Isaac Lamb, Pastor, Pennington-street, London
Richard Adams, Minister, Shad Thames, Southwark
Benjamin Keach, Pastor, Horse-lie-down, Southwark
Andrew Gifford, Pastor, Bristol, Frvars, Som. & Glouc.
Thomas Vaux, Pastor, Broadmead, Som. & Glouc.
Thomas Winnel, Pastor, Taunton, Som. & Glouc.
James Hitt, Preacher, Dalwood, Dorset
Richard Tidmarsh, Minister, Oxford City, Oxon
William Facey, Pastor, Reading, Berks

---

[1] *Arminianisim* takes its name from Jacob Arminius (1559-1609). He rejected the common Reformed views of predestination, free will, effectual calling, and a number of other issues (See Chapter 3, 5, 9). His followers would take up his mantle after his death and found many representatives in the days of the signatories of the *Second London Baptist Confession of Faith*. A group of Baptists commonly called General Baptists would be one such representative.

[2] *Meet* meaning proper or fitting.

Confessing Sound Words

Samuel Buttall, Minister, Plymouth, Devon
Christopher Price, Minister, Abergayenny, Monmouth
Daniel Finch, Minister, Kingsworth, Herts
John Ball, Tiverton, Devon
Edmond White, Pastor, Evershall, Bedford
William Prichard, Pastor, Blaenau, Monmouth
Paul Fruin, Minister, Warwick, Warwick
Richard Ring, Pastor, Southhampton, Hants
John Tomkins, Minister, Abingdon, Berks
Toby Willes, Pastor, Bridgewater, Somerset
John Carter, Steventon, Bedford
James Webb, Devizes, Wilts
Richard Sutton, Pastor, Tring, Herts
Robert Knight, Pastor, Stukeley, Bucks
Edward Price, Pastor, Hereford City, Hereford
William Phipps, Pastor, Exon, Devon
William Hawkins, Pastor, Dimmock, Gloucester
Samuel Ewer, Pastor, Hemstead, Herts
Edward Man, Pastor, Houndsditch, London
Charles Archer, Pastor, Hock-Norton, Oxon
In the name of and on the behalf of the whole assembly.

Appendix

Introduction

Whosoever reads, and impartially considers what we have in our forgoing confession declared, may readily perceive, that we do not only concenter[3] with all other true Christians on the Word of God (revealed in the Scriptures of truth) as the foundation and rule of our faith and worship. But that we have also industriously endeavored to manifest, that in the fundamental articles of Christianity we mind the same things, and have therefore expressed our belief in the same words, that have on the like occasion been spoken by other societies of Christians before us.

This we have done, that those who are desirous to know the principles of religion which we hold and practice, may take an estimate from our selves (who jointly

---

[3] *Concenter* meaning to agree.

Ending Statement, Signatories, and Appendix on Baptism

concur in this work) and may not be misguided, either by undue reports; or by the ignorance or errors of particular persons, who going under the same name with our selves, may give an occasion of scandalizing the truth we profess.

And although we do differ from our brethren who are paedobaptists;[4] in the subject and administration of baptism, and such other circumstances as have a necessary dependence on our observance of that ordinance, and do frequent our own assemblies for our mutual edification, and discharge of those duties, and services which we owe unto God, and in his fear to each other: yet we would not be from hence misconstrued, as if the discharge of our own consciences herein, did any ways disoblige or alienate our affections, or conversation from any others that fear the Lord; but that we may and do as we have opportunity participate of the labors of those, whom God has indued[5] with abilities above ourselves, and qualified, and called to the ministry of the Word, earnestly desiring to approve ourselves to be such, as follow after peace with holiness, and therefore we always keep that blessed *Irenicum*, or healing Word of the apostle before our eyes; "if in anything you be otherwise minded, God shall reveal even this unto you; nevertheless whereto we have already attained; let us walk by the same rule, let us mind the same thing" (Phil. 3:15, 16).

Let it not therefore be judged of us (because much has been written on this subject, and yet we continue this our practice different from others) that it is out of obstinacy, but rather as the truth is, that we do herein according to the best of our understandings worship God, out of a pure mind yielding obedience to his precept, in that method which we take to be most agreeable to the Scriptures of truth, and primitive practice.

It would not become us to give any such intimation, as should carry a semblance that what we do in the service of God is with a doubting conscience, or with any such temper of mind that we do thus for the present, with a reservation that we will do otherwise hereafter upon more mature deliberation; nor have we any cause so to do, being fully persuaded, that what we do is agreeable to the will of God. Yet we do heartily propose this, that if any of the servants of our Lord Jesus shall, in the spirit of meekness, attempt to convince us of any mistake either in judgement or practice, we shall diligently ponder his arguments; and account him our chiefest[6] friend that shall be an instrument to convert us from any error that is in our ways, for we cannot wittingly do anything against the truth, but all things for the truth.

---

[4] *Paedobaptists* meaning those who baptize infants.
[5] *Indued* meaning invested with a power or quality.
[6] *Chiefest* meaning best or greatest.

Confessing Sound Words

And therefore we have endeavored seriously to consider, what has been already offered for our satisfaction in this point; and are loath[7] to say any more lest we should be esteemed desirous of renewed contests about them: yet forasmuch as it may justly be expected that we show some reason, why we cannot acquiesce[8] in what has been urged against us; we shall with as much brevity as may consist with plainness, endeavor to satisfy the expectation of those that shall peruse what we now publish in this matter also.

1. Refutation of Historical Argument

As to those Christians who consent with us, that repentance from dead works, and faith towards God,[9] and our Lord Jesus Christ, is required in persons to be baptized; and do therefore supply the defect of the (infant being incapable of making confession of either) by others who do undertake these things for it. Although we do find by Church history that this has been a very ancient practice; yet considering, that the same Scripture which does caution us against censuring our brother, with whom "we shall all stand before the judgement seat of Christ," does also instruct us, that "every one of us shall give an account of himself to God," and "whatsoever is not of faith is sin" (Rom. 14:4, 10, 12, 23). Therefore we cannot for our own parts be persuaded in our own minds, to build such a practice as this, upon an unwritten tradition: but do rather choose in all points of faith and worship, to have recourse to the holy Scriptures, for the information of our judgement, and regulation of our practice; being well assured that a conscientious attending thereto, is the best way to prevent, and rectify our defects and errors (2 Tim. 3:16, 17). And if any such case happen to be debated between Christians, which is not plainly determinable by the Scriptures, we think it safest to leave such things undecided until the second coming of our Lord Jesus; as they did in the Church of old, until there should arise a priest with Urim and Thummim, that might certainly inform them of the mind of God thereabout (Ezra 2:62, 63).

2. Refutation of Covenantal and Circumcision Arguments

As for those our Christian brethren who do ground their arguments for infants' baptism, upon a presumed federal holiness, or church-membership, we conceive they are deficient in this, that albeit this covenant-holiness and membership should be as is supposed, in reference unto the infants of believers; yet no command for infant baptism does immediately and directly result from such a quality, or relation.

---

[7] *Loath* meaning reluctant.
[8] *Acquiesce* meaning remain quiet.
[9] Hebrews 6:1

All instituted worship receives its sanction from the precept, and is to be thereby governed in all the necessary circumstances thereof.

So it was in the covenant that God made with Abraham and his seed. The sign whereof was appropriated only to the male, notwithstanding that the female seed as well as the male were comprehended in the covenant and part of the church of God; neither was this sign to be affixed to any male infant till he was eight days old, albeit he was within the covenant from the first moment of his life; nor could the danger of death, or any other supposed necessity, warrant the circumcising of him before the set time, nor was there any cause for it; the commination[10] of being cut off from his people, being only upon the neglect, or contempt of the precept.

Righteous Lot was nearly related to Abraham in the flesh, and contemporary with him, when this covenant was made; yet inasmuch as he did not descend from his loins, nor was of his household family (although he was of the same household of faith with Abraham) yet neither Lot himself nor any of his posterity (because of their descent from him) were signed with the signature of this covenant that was made with Abraham and his seed.

This may suffice to show, that where there was both an express covenant, and a sign thereof (such a covenant as did separate the persons with whom it was made, and all their off-spring from all the rest of the world, as a people holy unto the Lord, and did constitute them the visible church of God, (though not comprehensive of all the faithful in the world) yet the sign of this Covenant was not affixed to all the persons that were within this Covenant, nor to any of them till the prefixed[11] season; nor to other faithful servants of God, that were not of descent from Abraham. And consequently, that it depends purely upon the will of the Lawgiver, to determine what shall be the sign of his covenant, unto whom, at what season, and upon what terms, it shall be affixed.

If our brethren do suppose baptism to be the seal of the covenant which God makes with every believer (of which the Scriptures are altogether silent) it is not our concern to contend with them herein; yet we conceive the seal of that covenant is the indwelling of the Spirit of Christ in the particular and individual persons in whom he resides, and nothing else, neither do they or we suppose that baptism is in any such manner substituted in the place of circumcision, as to have the same (and no other) latitude, extent, or terms, then circumcision had; for that was suited only for the male children, baptism is an ordinance suited for every believer, whether male, or female. That extended to all the males that were born in Abraham's house,

---

[10] *Commination* meaning denunciation of punishment.
[11] *Prefixed* meaning appointed.

or bought with his money, equally with the males that proceeded from his own loins; but baptism is not so far extended in any true Christian church that we know of, as to be administered to all the poor infidel[12] servants, that the members thereof purchase for their service, and introduce into their families; nor to the children born of them in their house.

But we conceive the same parity[13] of reasoning may hold for the ordinance of baptism as for that of circumcision (Exod. 12.49); viz.,[14] one law for the stranger, as for the home born: If any desire to be admitted to all the ordinances, and privileges of Gods house, the door is open; upon the same terms that any one person was ever admitted to all, or any of those privileges, that belong to the Christian church; may all persons of right challenge the like admission.

As for that text of Scripture, Romans 4:11, "He received circumcision a seal of the righteousness of the faith which he had yet being uncircumcised;" we conceive if the apostle's scope in that place be duly attended to, it will appear that no argument can be taken from thence to enforce infant baptism; and forasmuch as we find a full and fair account of those words given by the learned Dr. Lighfoot[15] (a man not to be suspected of partiality in this controversy) in his *Hor. Hebrai*,[16] (on 1 Cor. 7:19; pp. 42, 43), we shall transcribe his words at large, without any comment of our own upon them.

> Circumcision is nothing, if we respect the time, for now it was without use, that end of it being especially fulfilled; for which it had been instituted: this end the apostle declares in these words, (Rom. 4.11) σφραγιδα[17] etc. But I fear that by most translations they are not sufficiently suited to the end of circumcision, and the scope of the apostle whilst[18] something of their own is by them inserted.

And after the Doctor has represented diverse versions of the words agreeing for the most part in sense with that which we have in our Bibles, he thus proceeds.

> Other versions are to the same purpose; as if circumcision was given to Abraham for a seal of that righteousness which he had being yet

---

[12] *Infidel* meaning an unbeliever.
[13] *Parity* meaning similarity.
[14] *Viz.* meaning that is to say.
[15] John Lightfoot (1602-1675) was an English churchman, rabbinical scholar, prolific writer, and one of the Westminster Assembly divines.
[16] *Horae Hebraicae et Talmudicae* was a multi-volume commentary on Matthew, Mark, Luke, John, Acts, Romans, and 1 Corinthians.
[17] *Σφραγιδα* meaning seal.
[18] *Whilst* meaning while.

uncircumcised, which we will not deny to be in some sense true, but we believe that circumcision had chiefly a far different respect.

Give me leave thus to render the words; "And he received the sign of circumcision, a seal of the righteousness of faith, which was to be in the uncircumcision, which was to be," I say, not "which had been," not that which Abraham had whilst he was yet uncircumcised; but that which his uncircumcised seed should have, that is the Gentiles, who in time to come should imitate the faith of Abraham.

Now consider well on what occasion circumcision was instituted unto Abraham, setting before thine eyes the history thereof, (Gen. 17).

This promise is first made unto him, "Thou shalt be the Father of many Nations"[19] (in what sense the apostle explains in that chapter) and then there is subjoined a double seal for the confirmation of the thing, to wit,[20] the change of the name Abram into Abraham, and the institution of circumcision (17:4). "Behold as for me, my covenant is with thee, and thou shalt be the father of many nations." Wherefore[21] was his name called Abraham? For the sealing of this promise. "Thou shalt be the father of many nations." And wherefore was circumcision instituted to him? For the sealing of the same promise. "Thou shalt be the father of many nations." So that this is the sense of the apostle; most agreeable to the institution of circumcision; he received the sign of circumcision, a seal of the righteousness of faith which in time to come the uncircumcision (or the Gentiles) should have and obtain.

Abraham had a twofold seed, natural, of the Jews; and faithful, of the believing Gentiles: his natural seed was signed with the sign of circumcision, first indeed for the distinguishing of them from all other nations whilst they as yet were not the seed of Abraham, but especially for the memorial of the justification of the Gentiles by faith, when at length they should become his seed. Therefore, circumcision was of right to cease, when the Gentiles were brought in to the faith, forasmuch as then it had obtained its last and chief end, & thenceforth circumcision is nothing.

Thus far he, which we earnestly desire may be seriously weighed, for we plead not his authority, but the evidence of truth in his words.

---

[19] Genesis 17:4
[20] *To wit* meaning namely.
[21] *Wherefore* meaning why or for what reason.

3. Refutation of the Holiness Argument

Of whatsoever nature the holiness of the children mentioned [in] 1 Corinthians 7: 12 be, yet they who do conclude that all such children (whether infants or of riper years) have from hence an immediate right to baptism, do as we conceive put more into the conclusion, then will be found in the premises.

For although we do not determine positively concerning the apostle's scope in the holiness here mentioned, so as to say it is this, or that, and no other thing; yet it is evident that the apostle does by it determine not only the lawfulness but the expedience also of a believer's cohabitation with an unbeliever, in the state of marriage.

And we do think that although the apostle's asserting of the unbelieving yokefellow[22] to be sanctified by the believer, should carry in it somewhat more than is in the bare marriage of two infidels, because although the marriage covenant have a divine sanction so as to make the wedlock of two unbelievers a lawful action, and their conjunction and cohabitation in that respect undefiled, yet there might be no ground to suppose from thence, that both or either of their persons are thereby sanctified; and the apostle urges the cohabitation of a believer with an infidel in the state of wedlock from this ground that the unbelieving husband is sanctified by the believing wife; nevertheless here you have the influence of a believers faith ascending from an inferior to a superior relation; from the wife to the husband who is her head, before it can descend to their off-spring. And therefore we say, whatever be the nature or extent of the holiness here intended, we conceive it cannot convey to the children an immediate right to baptism; because it would then be of another nature, and of a larger extent, then the root, and original from whence it is derived, for it is clear by the apostle's argument that holiness cannot be derived to the child from the sanctity of one parent only, if either father or mother be (in the sense intended by the apostle) unholy or unclean, so will the child be also, therefore for the production of an holy seed it is necessary that both the parents be sanctified; and this the apostle positively asserts in the first place to be done by the believing parent, although the other be an unbeliever; and then consequentially from thence argues, the holiness of their children. Hence it follows, that as the children have no other holiness then what they derive from both their parents; so neither can they have any right by this holiness to any spiritual privilege but such as both their parents did also partake of: and therefore if the unbelieving parent (though sanctified by the believing parent) have not thereby a right to baptism, neither can we conceive, that there is any such privilege, derived to the children by their birth-holiness.

---

[22] *Yokefellow* meaning a spouse.

Besides if it had been the usual practice in the apostle's days for the father or mother that did believe, to bring all their children with them to be baptized; then the holiness of the believing Corinthians' children, would not at all have been in question when this epistle was written; but might have been argued from their passing under that ordinance, which represented their new birth, although they had derived no holiness from their parents, by their first birth; and would have lain as an exception against the apostle's inference, "else were your children unclean..."[23] But of the sanctification of all the children of every believer by this ordinance, or any other way, then what is before mentioned, the Scripture is altogether silent.

This may also be added; that if this birth holiness do qualify all the children of every believer, for the ordinance of baptism; why not for all other ordinances? For the Lord's Supper as was practiced for a long time together. For if recourse be had to what the Scriptures speak generally of this subject; it will be found, that the same qualities which do entitle any person to baptism, do so also for the participation of all the ordinances, and privileges of the house of God, that are common to all believers.

Whosoever can and does interrogate his good conscience towards God when he is baptized (as everyone must do that makes it to himself a sign of Salvation) is capable of doing the same thing, in every other act of worship that he performs.

4. Refutation of Household Baptism Argument and Other Arguments

The arguments and inferences that are usually brought for, or against infant baptism from those few instances which the Scriptures afford us of whole families being baptized; are only conjectural; and therefore cannot of themselves, be conclusive on either hand: yet in regard most that treat on this subject for infant baptism, do (as they conceive) improve these instances to the advantage of their argument: we think it meet[24] (in like manner as in the cases before mentioned so in this) to show the invalidity of such inferences.

"Cornelius worshipped God with all his house,"[25] the jailer, and Crispus the chief ruler of the Synagogue, "believed God with each of their houses." The household of Stephanus[26] addicted themselves to the ministry of the saints: so that thus far worshiping, and believing runs parallel with baptism. And if Lydia, had been a married person, when she believed, it is probable her husband would also have been

---

[23] 1 Corinthians 7:14.
[24] Acts 10:44.
[25] Acts 16:34; 18:8.
[26] 1 Corinthians 1:16; 16:15.

named by the apostle, as in like cases, inasmuch as he would have been not only a part, but the head of that baptized household.[27]

Who can assign any probable reason, why the apostle should make mention of four or five households being baptized and no more or why he does so often vary in the method of his salutations (Rom. 1:6) sometimes mentioning only particular persons of great note, other times such, and the church in their house? The saints that were with them; and them belonging to Narcissus,[28] who were in the Lord; thus saluting either whole families, or part of families, or only particular persons in families, considered as they were in the Lord, for if it had been an usual practice to baptize all children, with their parents; there were then many thousands of the Jews which believed, and a great number of the Gentiles, in most of the principle cities in the world, and among so many thousands, it is more than probable there would have been some thousands of households baptized; why then should the apostle in this respect signalize one family of the Jews and three or four of the Gentiles, as particular instances in a case that was common? Whoever supposes that we do willfully debar[29] our children, from the benefit of any promise, or privilege, that of right belongs to the children of believing parents; they do entertain over severe thoughts of us: to be without natural affections is one of the characters of the worst of persons; in the worst of times. We do freely confess ourselves guilty before the Lord, in that we have not with more circumspection and diligence trained up those that relate to us in the fear of the Lord; and do humbly and earnestly pray, that our omissions herein may be remitted, and that they may not redound to the prejudice of ourselves, or any of ours: but with respect to that duty that is incumbent on us, we acknowledge ourselves obliged by the precepts of God, to bring up our children in the nurture and admonition of the Lord, to teach them his fear, both by instruction and example; and should we set light by this precept, it would demonstrate that we are more vile then the unnatural heathen, that like not to retain God in their knowledge, our baptism might then be justly accounted, as no baptism to us.

There are many special promises that do encourage us as well as precepts, that do oblige us to the close pursuit of our duty herein: that God whom we serve, being jealous of his worship, threatens the visiting of the fathers' transgression upon the children to the third and fourth generation of them that hate him:[30] yet does more

---

[27] Acts 16:14-15.
[28] Romans 16:11.
[29] *Debar* meaning to exclude.
[30] Exodus 20:5.

abundantly extend his mercy, even to thousands (respecting the offspring and succeeding generations) of them that love him, and keep his commands.[31]

When our Lord rebuked his disciples for prohibiting the access of little children that were brought to him, that he might pray over them, lay his hands upon them, and bless them, does declare, "that of such is the Kingdom of God."[32] And the apostle Peter in answer to their inquiry, that desired to know what they must do to be saved, does not only instruct them in the necessary duty of repentance and baptism; but does also thereto encourage them, by that promise which had reference both to them, and their children;[33] if our Lord Jesus in the forementioned place, do not respect the qualities of children (as elsewhere) as to their meekness, humility, and sincerity, and the like; but intend also that those very persons and such like, appertain to the Kingdom of God, and if the apostle Peter in mentioning the aforesaid promise, do respect not only the present and succeeding generations of those Jews, that heard him, (in which sense the same phrase does occur in Scripture) but also the immediate off-spring of his auditors; whether the promise relate to the gift of the Holy Spirit, or of eternal life, or any grace, or privilege tending to the obtaining thereof; it is neither our concern nor our interest to confine the mercies, and promises of God, to a more narrow, or lesser compass then he is pleased graciously to offer and intend them; nor to have a light esteem of them; but are obliged in duty to God, and affection to our children; to plead earnestly with God and use our utmost endeavors that both ourselves, and our off-spring may be partakers of his mercies and gracious promises: yet we cannot from either of these texts collect a sufficient warrant for us to baptize our children before they are instructed in the principles of the Christian religion.

For as to the instance in little children, it seems by the disciples forbidding them, that they were brought upon some other account, not so frequent as baptism must be supposed to have been, if from the beginning believers children had been admitted thereto: and no account is given whether their parents were baptized believers or not; and as to the instance of the apostle; if the following words and practice, may be taken as an interpretation of the scope of that promise we cannot conceive it does refer to infant baptism, because the text does presently subjoin; "Then they that gladly received the word were baptized."[34]

That there were some believing children of believing parents in the apostle's days is evident from the Scriptures, even such as were then in their fathers family,

---

[31] Exodus 20:6.
[32] Mark 10:14.
[33] Acts 2:38–39.
[34] Acts 2:41.

and under their parents tuition, and education; to whom the apostle in several of his epistles to the churches, gives commands to obey their parents in the Lord; and does allure their tender years to hearken to this precept, by reminding them that it is the first command with promise.[35]

And it is recorded by him for the praise of Timothy, and encouragement of parents betimes to instruct, and children early to attend to godly instruction, that απο βρεφος "from a child," he had known the holy Scriptures.[36]

The apostle John rejoiced greatly when he found of the children of the elect lady walking in the truth; and the children of her elect sister join with the apostle in his salutation.[37]

But that this was not generally so, that all the children of believers were accounted for believers (as they would have been if they had been all baptized) may be collected from the character which the apostle gives of persons fit to be chosen to eldership in the church which was not common to all believers; among others this is expressly one, viz. "If there be any having believing, or faithful children,"[38] not accused of riot or unruly; and we may from the apostle's writings on the same subject collect the reason of this qualification, viz. That in case the person designed for this office to teach and rule in the house of God, had children capable of it; there might be first a proof of his ability, industry, and success in this work in his own family; and private capacity, before he was ordained to the exercise of this authority in the church, in a public capacity, as a bishop in the house of God.

These things we have mentioned as having a direct reference unto the controversy between our brethren and us; other things that are more abstruse[39] and prolix,[40] which are frequently introduced into this controversy, but do not necessarily concern it, we have purposely avoided; that the distance between us and our brethren may not be by us made more wide; for it is our duty, and concern so far as is possible for us (retaining a good conscience towards God) to seek a more entire agreement and reconciliation with them.

We are not insensible that as to the order of God's house, and entire communion therein there are some things wherein we (as well as others) are not at a full accord among ourselves, as for instance; the known principle, and state of the consciences of diverse of us, that have agreed in this confession is such; that we cannot hold church-communion, with any other then baptized believers, and churches

---

[35] Ephesians 6:2.
[36] 2 Timothy 3:15.
[37] 2 John 1–4.
[38] Titus 1:6.
[39] *Abstruse* meaning difficult to understand.
[40] *Porlix* meaning wordy.

constituted of such; yet some others of us have a greater liberty and freedom in our spirits that way; and therefore we have purposely omitted the mention of things of that nature, that we might concur, in giving this evidence of our agreement, both among ourselves, and with other good Christians, in those important articles of the Christian religion, mainly insisted on by us: and this notwithstanding we all esteem it our chief concern, both among ourselves, and all others that in every place call upon the name of the Lord Jesus Christ our Lord, both theirs and ours, and love him in sincerity, to endeavor "to keep the unity of the Spirit, in the bond of peace;"[41] and in order thereunto, to exercise "all lowliness and meekness, with long-suffering, forbearing one another in love."[42]

And we are persuaded if the same method were introduced into frequent practice between us and our Christian friends who agree with us in all the fundamental articles of the Christian faith (though they do not so in the subject and administration of baptism), it would soon beget a better understanding, and brotherly affection between us.

Conclusion

In the beginning of the Christian Church, when the doctrine of the baptism of Christ was not universally understood, yet those that knew only the baptism of John, were the disciples of the Lord Jesus; and Apollos an eminent minister of the gospel of Jesus.

In the beginning of the reformation of the Christian Church, and recovery from that Egyptian darkness wherein our forefathers for many generations were held in bondage; upon recourse had to the Scriptures of truth, different apprehensions were conceived, which are to this time continued, concerning the practice of this ordinance.

Let not our zeal herein be misinterpreted: that God whom we serve is jealous of his worship. By his gracious providence, the law thereof, is continued amongst us; and we are forewarned by what happened in the Church of the Jews, that it is necessary for every generation, and that frequently in every generation to consult the divine oracle, compare our worship with the rule, and take heed to what doctrines we receive and practice.

If the ten commands exhibited in the popish idolatrous service books had been received as the entire law of God, because they agree in number with his ten commands, and also in the substance of nine of them; the second Commandment forbidding idolatry had been utterly lost.

---

[41] Ephesians 4:3.
[42] Ephesians 4:6.

If Ezra and Nehemiah had not made a diligent search into the particular parts of God's law, and his worship; the Feast of Tabernacles (which for many centuries of years, had not been duly observed, according to the institution, though it was retained in the general notion) would not have been kept in due order.

So may it be now as to many things relating to the service of God, which do retain the names proper to them in their first institution, but yet through inadvertency (where there is no sinister design) may vary in their circumstances, from their first institution. And if by means of any ancient defection, or of that general corruption of the service of God, and interruption of his true worship, and persecution of his servants by the antichristian bishop of Rome, for many generations; those who do consult the Word of God, cannot yet arrive at a full and mutual satisfaction among themselves, what was the practice of the primitive Christian Church, in some points relating to the worship of God: yet inasmuch as these things are not of the essence of Christianity, but that we agree in the fundamental doctrines thereof, we do apprehend, there is sufficient ground to lay aside all bitterness and prejudice, and in the spirit of love and meekness to embrace and own each other therein; leaving each other at liberty to perform such other services, (wherein we cannot concur) apart unto God, according to the best of our understanding.

FINIS

Acknowledgements

This book has been in my mind since I began my pastorate at Vista Baptist Church in 2017. The willingness of two men to meet me weekly for discipleship motivated me to put what was in my mind to writing. Thank you, Daniel Wisner and Samuel Smart, for journeying through the earliest parts and versions of this curriculum. I also would like to thank my wife, Lauren. She has supported me faithfully and prayerfully in every endeavour I take. Thank you, Austin McCormick, Ryan Pendergraft, Jake Stone, and Dewey Dovel, for giving me feedback and encouragement throughout the writing process. Lastly, thank you to the men and women who have poured into me throughout my life. Of said people, a special thanks go to my mother, Lisa Brandenburg, my youth pastor Jeremy Bundren, my resident director from college Brandon Van Marel, and my college pastor and professor, Dr. John Greever.

Bibliography

The Baptist Confession of Faith & The Baptist Catechism. Vestavia Hills, AL: Solid Ground Christian Books, 2014.

DeRouchie, Jason Shane. *How to Understand and Apply the Old Testament: Twelve Steps from Exegesis to Theology.* Phillipsburg, NJ: P & R Publishing, 2017.

Helm, David R. *One to One Bible Reading: A Simple Guide for Every Christian.* Sydney, NSW: Matthias Media, 2020.

Naselli, Andrew David. *How to Understand and Apply the New Testament: Twelve Steps from Exegesis to Theology.* Phillipsburg, NJ: P & R Publishing, 2017.

Renihan, James M., ed. *Faith and Life for Baptists: the Documents of the London Particular Baptist General Assemblies, 1689-1694.* Palmdale, CA: Reformed Baptist Academic Press, 2016.

Sproul, R. C. *Truths We Confess: A Systematic Exposition of the Westminster Confession of Faith.* Sanford, FL: Reformation Trust Publishing, 2019.

Van Dixhoorn, Chad. *Confessing the Faith: A Reader's Guide to the Westminster Confession of Faith.* Edinburgh: Banner of Truth Trust, 2014.

Watson, Thomas. *The Select Works of the Rev. Thomas Watson: Comprising His Celebrated Body of Divinity, in a Series of Lectures on the Shorter Catechism, and Various Sermons and Treatises.* New York: Robert Cater & Brothers, 1855.

Scripture Index

Old Testament

Genesis
- 1 43
- 1:1 46
- 1:20 53
- 1:26 .... 45, 47
- 1:26–28 43
- 1:27 .... 45, 47, 145
- 1:28 181
- 1:31 47
- 2:3 46
- 2:4–25 .... 44, 52
- 2:7 47
- 2:16 .... 51, 58, 61
- 2:16–17 52
- 2:17 .... 47, 49, 51, 58, 61, 68
- 2:18 181
- 2:24 181
- 3 150
- 3:6 .... 47, 57, 84
- 3:6–8 57
- 3:8 59
- 3:10 59
- 3:12 .... 57, 62
- 3:13 62
- 3:15 .... 69, 151
- 3:19 225
- 3:24 59
- 4:5 127
- 6:5 62
- 8:22 53
- 17 241
- 17:1 31
- 17:4 241
- 28:20–22 172
- 50:1 38
- 50:15–21 .... 38, 50

Exodus
- 3:14 .... 27, 30, 32
- 8:5 6
- 8:15,32 54
- 12 240
- 15:1–19 167
- 16:25–28 162
- 20:1–21 .... 142, 165
- 20:3 5
- 20:4 217
- 20:4–6 166
- 20:5 .... 217, 244
- 20:6 245
- 20:7 171
- 20:8 .... 162, 165, 167
- 20:8–11 .... 161, 165
- 20:9,11 163
- 20:10 162
- 20:12 173
- 21:13 53
- 34:6 27
- 34:6,7 31
- 34:7 31

Leviticus
- 10:1–19 163
- 18 182
- 19:12 171

Numbers
- 23:19 38

Deuteronomy
- 2:30 54
- 4:15,16 31
- 5:12–14 161
- 5:12–15 165
- 5:16 174
- 6:1–9 30
- 6:1–25 170
- 6:4 .... 27, 29, 30
- 6:13 170
- 10:4 .... 141, 145
- 10:12–21 169
- 10:20 171
- 12:29 165
- 12:32 .... 165, 166
- 13:18 165
- 19:5 53
- 26:17 5
- 29:4 54
- 30:6 91
- 30:11–20 82
- 30:19 .... 82, 84

1 Samuel
- 15:22 141

2 Samuel
- 7:29 166
- 12:14 133
- 12:21–23 166
- 23:3 177
- 24:1 53

1 Kings
- 8:27 31
- 21:27,29 127
- 22:28,34 53

2 Kings
- 8:12 54
- 10:30 127
- 19:28 53

1 Chronicles
- 21:1 53
- 28:9 5

2 Chronicles
- 6:22,23 171
- 32:25 54
- 32:26 54
- 32:31 54

Ezra
- 2:62 238
- 2:63 238

Nehemiah
- 8:8 201
- 9:32,33 31
- 13:15–22 .... 162, 167
- 13:25 171
- 13:25–27 181

Esther
- 4:16 167

Job
- 8:13,14 137
- 9:2,3 126
- 11:7,8,9 27
- 14:4 62
- 19:26,27 .... 221, 226
- 21:14,15 127
- 22:2,3 31
- 26:13 47
- 35:7 68
- 35:8 68
- 38:11 52

Psalms
- 1:21 54
- 2:6 .... 71, 76
- 2:8–11 71
- 5:5 31
- 5:6 31
- 14:1 .... 5, 11, 13
- 19 20
- 19:1,2,3 19
- 19:1–3 23
- 19:7 25
- 19:8 201
- 24:4 171
- 27:7–10 114
- 29:2 5
- 30:7 139
- 31:22 138
- 32:3,4 133
- 40:7 77
- 40:8 77
- 42:5,11 139
- 45:7 77
- 49:14 222
- 51:5 62
- 51:8,12,14 138
- 51:10,12 133
- 55:17 167
- 65:2 166
- 72:17 189
- 76:10 53
- 76:11 172
- 77:1–12,88 138
- 77:7,8 138
- 81:10 5
- 81:11 5
- 81:11,12 54
- 82:3,4 177
- 89:31,32 132
- 89:31–33 97
- 90:2 31
- 95:1–7 166
- 97:9 11
- 102:28 189
- 103 51
- 103:13 102
- 103:19 .... 49, 51
- 104:24 49
- 107 167
- 110:1 79
- 110:2 27
- 110:3 .... 68, 79, 91, 152
- 115:3 31
- 116:11 138
- 116:12,13 126
- 118:24 161
- 119:6,128 120
- 119:11,18 202
- 119:32 138
- 119:68 31
- 119:72 114
- 119:130 25
- 122:6 191
- 135:6 52
- 143:2 127
- 145:17 .... 31, 49
- 147:5 27
- 147:20 152
- 148:13 31

Proverbs
- 2:1–6 111
- 4:18 129
- 8:34 202
- 14:26 102

Ending Statement, Signatories, and Appendix on Baptism

16:4	31
16:33	53
22:19-21	23
29:18	152
30:5	208

Ecclesiastes

7:20	62, 120
7:29	47, 57, 84, 145
12:7	226
12:14	231

Song of Solomon

1:4	91
5:2-3,6	138

Isaiah

1:16,17	117
1:16-18	120
6:3	31
6:9	54
6:10	54
8:20	23, 25
9:6	71
9:7	71
10:5-7	38
10:6,7,12	53
25:7	152
26:3,4	111
28:29	49
29:13	126
32:1	72
32:2	72
32:33	72
40:9-31	11
42:1	76
43:3-5	54
44	13
44:6	11, 13
46:10	31, 35, 38, 52
48:12	11, 30
50:10	138
53:2	73
53:3	73
53:5	96
53:6	78, 96
53:10	76
54:8	102
54:9	102
55:2,3	111
55:7	120
55:10,11	53
57:2	221
58:13	162, 167
60:2,3	152
64:5,9	133
64:6	127
64:7	126
66:2	114
66:23	162

Jeremiah

3:22	117
4:2	171
10:7	166
10:10	27, 30
17:9	62
17:24-27	162
23:10	171
23:23	31
31:18,19	117
31:31-37	67
31:33	67
31:35	53
32:40	132

Lamentations

3:26-31	139
3:31	102
3:37	35, 37
3:38	37
3:39	59

Ezekiel

11:5	31
22:26	162
23:38	162
34:2-4	173
36:22-37	117
36:26	68, 87, 91
36:27	68, 87, 91, 146
36:31	117, 120

Daniel

3:27	53
4:25,34,35	31

Hosea

1:6	53
1:7	53

Joel

2:12	117, 167

Amos

5:21,22	127
8:5	162
9:8,9	54

Micah

6:8	126, 141

Nahum

1:2,3	31

Zechariah

12:10	120

Malachi

1:11	167
1:13	162
2:15	181
3:6	31, 132

New Testament

Matthew
- 1:22 ... 75
- 1:23 ... 75
- 3:6 ... 203
- 3:11 ... 198
- 3:13–17 ... 28
- 3:15 ... 75
- 3:16 ... 204, 207
- 4:9,10 ... 162
- 4:10 ... 5
- 5:16 ... 122
- 5:17–19 ... 141
- 5:34,37 ... 167
- 6:2,5 ... 123
- 6:6 ... 163
- 6:11 ... 163
- 6:12 ... 95
- 6:30 ... 110
- 7:6 ... 214
- 7:22,23 ... 133
- 10:29–31 ... 47, 50
- 10:32 ... 217
- 12:1–13 ... 158, 163
- 12:36 ... 227
- 12:40 ... 71
- 13:12 ... 52
- 13:20 ... 89
- 15:4–6 ... 169
- 15:9 ... 122, 154, 213
- 15:19 ... 56, 60
- 16:18 ... 185
- 17:9–13 ... 79
- 17:12 ... 82
- 18:15–17 ... 187
- 18:15–20 ... 181, 185
- 18:17,18 ... 185
- 19:1–12 ... 175
- 19:5,6 ... 177
- 19:11 ... 168
- 19:17–19 ... 137
- 21:5 ... 69
- 22:14 ... 89
- 22:23–40 ... 140
- 22:29,31,32 ... 25
- 22:37–39 ... 140
- 22:37–40 ... 138
- 25:21,23 ... 123
- 25:21,34 ... 228
- 25:23 ... 217
- 25:31–46 ... 225
- 25:32–46 ... 227
- 25:34 ... 38
- 25:41 ... 57
- 25:41,46 ... 218
- 25:41-43 ... 123
- 25:46 ... 57, 228
- 26:26 ... 213
- 26:26–28 ... 209, 213
- 26:27 ... 213
- 26:37 ... 76
- 26:38 ... 69
- 26:70,72,74 ... 128
- 26:75 ... 95
- 27:46 ... 71, 76
- 28:1 ... 157
- 28:1–10 ... 200
- 28:16–20 ... 200
- 28:18 ... 75
- 28:18–20 ... 185, 200
- 28:19 ... 27, 32, 162, 197, 201, 203, 207
- 28:19,20 ... 201, 204
- 28:20 ... 162, 185, 197, 207

Mark
- 1:4 ... 203, 207
- 2:27,28 ... 157
- 6:18 ... 178
- 9:48 ... 228
- 10:1–12 ... 176
- 10:1–31 ... 176
- 10:4 ... 176
- 10:6–9 ... 176
- 10:14 ... 241
- 12:33 ... 161
- 13:35-37 ... 228
- 16:2 ... 157
- 16:15 ... 66
- 16:16 ... 66, 203, 207
- 16:19 ... 71, 76

Luke
- 1:6 ... 181
- 1:27 ... 69, 75
- 1:31 ... 69, 75
- 1:33 ... 74
- 1:34 ... 69
- 1:35 ... 69, 75
- 1:42 ... 69
- 1:73–75 ... 154
- 1:74 ... 77
- 1:75 ... 77
- 2:7 ... 71
- 3:7 ... 204
- 3:14 ... 173
- 4:16 ... 158
- 8:15 ... 198
- 8:18 ... 162
- 10:20 ... 39

Ending Statement, Signatories, and Appendix on Baptism

12:35-40	228
16:19-31	220
16:22	220
16:23	220
16:23,24	218, 222
16:29	23
16:31	23
17:5	110
17:10	66, 122
19:8	116
22:31,32	116
22:32	134
22:32,61,62	129
22:44	71, 76
23:26-43	220
23:43	217, 220, 222
24:1	157
24:6	213
24:27	24
24:30-36	157
24:39	213
24:44	24

John
1:1-18	99
1:2,3	45
1:11-13	71
1:12	94, 97, 99, 100, 107, 110
1:13	99
1:14	69, 75, 99
1:14,18	32
1:16	193
1:18	70, 77
3:1-21	108
3:3	89
3:5	89
3:6	89
3:8	77, 89
3:13	76
3:16	66
3:23	204, 207
3:34	75
4:21	163
4:22	89
4:24	27, 30
5:19-29	221
5:22	75
5:22,27	227
5:25	89
5:26	31
5:27	75
5:28	220, 221, 222
5:28,29	222
5:28,29	218
5:29	220, 221
5:38	20
5:39	25
6:1-15	87
6:22-59	87
6:23	162
6:35	87
6:37	71, 76
6:39	71
6:44	66, 82, 85, 87, 88, 89, 148
6:45	24, 66, 85, 87, 89
6:64	39
6:65	89
7:38,39	154
8:12	87
8:36	82
8:56	67
10:7-9	87
10:11	87
10:15	76
10:16	76, 185
10:18	75
10:22-42	125, 127
10:26	39, 127
10:27	127
10:28	95, 127
10:28,29	128
10:29	127
11:25	87
12:32	185
13:18	39
14:6	87, 162
14:11	32
14:13,14	162
14:14	110
14:19	128
15:1-5	87
15:4,5	122
15:15	70
15:26	32
16:8	77
16:13	24
16:14	24
17:2	76
17:3	89
17:6	74, 77
17:9	39, 77
17:17	104
17:17-19	20
19:11	38
20:1	157
20:19-21	157
20:25	76
20:27	76
20:31	70

Acts
1:3	157
1:8	206
1:9-11	76
1:11	71, 76
1:25	218
2:1,2	157
2:14-38	204

Reference	Pages
2:14–41	115
2:23	51
2:24–27	71
2:31	71
2:36	75
2:37	85, 115
2:37,38	113, 203
2:38	115, 203
2:38-39	241
2:41	185, 207, 241
2:41,42	181, 209
2:42	163, 183, 185, 197
2:42–47	183
2:46	197
2:47	197
3:21	213
3:22	69, 74
3:38	204
4:12	67, 89
4:19,29	154
4:27,28	38
5:4	194
5:13	185
5:13,14	181
5:14	185
6:3	186
6:4	186
8:12,36,37	207
8:26–40	206
8:30	20
8:36	206
8:36–38	203
8:38	206, 207
9:26	181
10:2	163
10:7	158
10:38	75
10:42	76
10:44	239
10:48	204
11:18	116
11:19–21	186
11:26	184
11:28	113
11:29	194
11:30	194
13:36	221
13:37	76
14:23	186
15:2	187
15:4	187
15:6	187
15:11	110
15:15	25
15:15,16	25
15:18	31, 38
15:22	187
15:23	187
15:25	187
15:14–16	70
16:7	148
16:14-15	239
16:31	110
16:34	239
17:11	16
17:24	19
17:31	71, 74, 227
18:8	207, 239
20:7	157, 158, 163
20:17,28	186
20:21	107
20:28	76
20:32	104, 110, 197
22:16	203, 207
24:14	110
24:15	222
26:18	85, 89, 154, 197
27:31,44	51
28:23	25

Romans
Reference	Pages
1:1–17	147
1:6	240
1:7	184, 185
1:12	193
1:15,16	197
1:16	65, 88, 99, 103, 140, 146, 147
1:16–17	58, 206
1:17	65, 88, 99, 103, 140, 146, 147
1:18	58, 65, 88, 99, 103, 140, 206
1:18–32	148
1:19,20	19
1:19-21	23
1:20	45
1:21	6
1:24	52
1:25	6, 162
1:26	6, 52
2:14	23
2:14,15	45, 137, 141
2:15	23
3:1–26	140
3:2	24, 25
3:10–19	60
3:20	58, 65, 66, 88, 99, 103, 122, 140, 142, 206
3:20–22	63
3:21	58, 65, 66, 88, 99, 103, 206
3:21-31	91
3:23	60
3:24	91, 94
3:25	76
3:26	76, 94

Ending Statement, Signatories, and Appendix on Baptism

Reference	Page
3:28	94
3:31	141
4	236
4:1	67
4:2	67
4:5–8	94
4:6	123
4:6–8	91
4:11	236
4:19,20	110
4:19-21	51
4:19–21	51
4:22	95
4:24	95
4:25	95
5:1,2,5	134
5:1,2,5,17	125
5:2,5	134
5:6	82
5:9,10	128
5:10	77
5:12	56, 57, 58, 60
5:12–19	60
5:12–21	47, 50, 56, 57, 58
5:17	94
5:17–19	91, 94
5:21	58, 65, 88, 99, 103, 206
6:1	134
6:1,2	154
6:1–14	101, 206
6:2	134, 207
6:3	206
6:3–5	203, 207
6:4	101, 204, 206
6:5	193
6:5,6	104
6:6	101, 193
6:12–14	142
6:14	104, 142
6:20	60
6:22	122
6:23	57, 116
6–8	65, 88, 99, 103, 206
7:7	142
7:15	82
7:18	60, 82
7:18,23	104
7:19	82
7:21	82
7:23	60, 82, 104
7:23–25	60
8:1	142
8:1–11	66
8:1–17	99
8:3	65, 66, 75, 154
8:4	65
8:7	60, 82
8:9	77
8:14	77, 97, 99
8:15	100, 154
8:15,16	134
8:17	100
8:18–30	88, 103
8:26	162
8:28	38, 52, 53, 88, 154
8:28–30	88, 103
8:29	103
8:30	39, 74, 85, 87, 88, 94, 128
8:32	94
8:34	76
9:5	69, 75
9:11,13,16,18	38
9:11,16	128
9:13	39
9:15,18	38
9:16	39, 123
9:22,23	35, 39, 227
10:4	142
10:5	137, 141
10:13–17	197
10:14,15,17	147
10:14,17	110
11:5	39
11:6	39
11:7	52, 88
11:8	52
11:20	39
11:32	51
11:33	39
11:34	51
11:34–36	31
11:36	31, 147
12:10	169
12–16	58
13:1–4	173
13:1–7	170
13:5–7	173
13:8	169
13:8–10	141
14:4	154, 234
14:9	76
14:10	76, 234
14:10, 12	227
14:12	234
14:17	134
14:23	234
15:4	23, 197
16:1	187
16:2	187
16:11	240
1 Corinthians	
1:2	184, 185
1:9	71
1:16	239
1:30	85, 94
1:31	94

2:9-12	24
2:10-12	24
2:14	89, 148
3:5	154
3:6,7	198
3:21-23	193
4:1	201
4:10	76
5	184
5:1	178
5:4,5,13	185
5:7	141, 210
5:8	210
6:3	227
7:2,9	167, 177
7:12	237
7:14	239
7:19	236
7:23	154
7:39	177
8:4,6	30
8:6	32
9:6-14	186
9:8-10	141
10:1-22	212
10:16	209, 210, 212, 213, 214
10:17	210, 212, 213
10:21	213
11:13,14	24
11:17-33	210, 212
11:17-34	201
11:23	200
11:23-26	209, 213, 214
11:24	213
11:24,25	214
11:26	162, 201
11:26-28	213
11:27	213
11:28	210, 212
11:29	210, 212, 214
11:31	210
11:32	128
12:3	198
12:7	193
12:12-31	191
12:14-27	194
13:1	123
13:12	217
14:6,9,11,12,24,28	25
14:16	162
14:24	197
14:25	197
14:26,40	24
15:1-11	145
15:3	76
15:4	71, 76
15:12-28	218
15:21	56, 60
15:22	56, 60
15:25	70, 77
15:26	77
15:42,43	222
15:43	217
15:45	60
15:49	60
15:50-58	221
15:51	220, 221
15:51,52	222
15:52	220, 221
15:54-57	154
16:1	163
16:1,2	157
16:15	239

2 Corinthians

1:23	167
1:24	154, 187
2:6-8	185
3:1-18	151
3:5	122
3:18	104
4:4,6	148
4:13	110
5:1,6,8	217, 222
5:1-10	226
5:10	226, 227
5:10,11	228
5:19	91
5:21	76, 91, 94
6:14,15	214
6:18	100
7:1	104
7:11	113, 116
9:13	185
11:3	60
12:7-9	52
13:3	69
13:5	210
13:14	27, 29, 30, 32

Galatians

1:4	154
1:6-9	93, 152, 193
1:8,9	24
2:15-21	93
2:16	91, 93, 107, 142
2:20	110
3:8	95
3:9	95
3:9,14	154
3:10	57, 66
3:10,12	141
3:10-14	153
3:12	47

3:13	75, 152, 154	3:16–19	104
3:14	152	3:17	71
3:21	63, 142	4:2,3	187
3:22	63	4:3	243
3:27	203, 207	4:6	243
4:1–7	97	4:11	185
4:4	69, 71, 75, 100	4:13	82
4:5	100	4:15,16	104, 193
4:6	32, 100	4:23	101
5:6	94	4:24	41, 101
5:13	154	4:28	167, 194
5:17	60, 77, 104, 122	4:30	100, 128
5:22,23	123	5:19	162
5:24	104	5:21	169
6:1–10	193	5:23	184
6:2	192	5:27	184
6:6,7	186	5:32	184
6:10	192, 193	6:2	242

Ephesians

1:3-5	38	6:2,3	170
1:3–14	35	6:4	194
1:4	63	6:16	111
1:4,9,11	39	6:18	187

Philippians

1:4,11	35	1:1	186
1:5	39, 63, 85, 100	1:3-11	127
1:6	39, 94, 123	1:6	127, 128
1:7	94	1:11	122
1:8	77	1:23	217, 222
1:9	77	2:5–11	72
1:10	88, 184	2:8	71
1:11	38, 50, 88	2:12	103, 122
1:13	71	2:12-13	103
1:14	71	2:12-18	103
1:17	89	2:13	82, 85, 103, 122
1:18	89	3:1-11	109
1:19	89	3:8	94, 109
1:19,20	148	3:8-9	109
1:20	71, 89	3:9	91, 94, 107, 109
1:20–22	184	3:10	193
1:22	74, 184	3:15	233
1:23	74, 184	3:16	233
2:1	80, 81, 82	3:21	222

Colossians

2:1–3	56	1:11	104
2:1–6	89	1:13	82
2:1–10	36, 81, 121	1:15–23	183
2:2	57	1:16	45
2:3	57, 60	1:18	183, 184, 185
2:5	39, 82, 89	1:19	75
2:7	94	1:21	60, 77, 95
2:8	71, 89, 110	1:22	95
2:8,9	122	2:2	111
2:8–10	94, 120, 121	2:3	75
2:10	122	2:9	69
2:12	39	2:12	203, 204, 207
2:14	141	2:14	141
2:16	141	2:16	141
2:18	100	2:17	141
2:20	19, 23, 25		

2:18 162
2:20,22,23 154
3:10 41
3:16 .... 25, 162

1 Thessalonians
   1:4 39
   1:5 39
   1:10 60
   4:14 217
   4:17 .... 217, 222
   4:18 217
   5:9 39
   5:10 39
   5:11 193
   5:14 .... 186, 193
   5:21-23 104
   5:23 104

2 Thessalonians
   1:5-7 228
   1:7-10 228
   1:8 218
   1:9 218
   1:10 154
   2:2-9 185
   2:10 198
   2:10-12 52
   2:11 184
   2:12 184
   2:13 .... 24, 39, 85, 88, 101
   2:13-17 86
   2:14 .... 85, 88
   3:6,14,15 186

1 Timothy
   1:13,15 116
   1:17 30
   2:1 .... 162, 172
   2:1,2 173
   2:1-2 172
   2:1-15 172
   2:2 .... 162, 172
   2:5 .... 69, 75, 77, 162
   2:6 .... 69, 95
   2:8 163
   3:2 186
   4:3 177
   4:10 52
   4:13 162
   4:14 186
   5:17,18 186
   5:21 38
   6:1 122

2 Timothy
   1:9 39, 67, 85, 89
   1:12 110
   1:13 20
   2:4 186

2:19 .... 39, 128
3:1-17 198
3:15 242
3:15,16 .... 19, 20
3:15-17 .... 23, 24, 197
3:16 .... 19, 22, 24, 234
3:17 .... 22, 234
4:2 162
4:8 228

Titus
   1:2 67
   1:6 242
   1:15 60
   2:11 134
   2:12 134
   2:14 134
   3:2-5 116
   3:3-5 82
   3:4-7 95
   3:5 .... 71, 123
   3:6 71

Hebrews
   1:1 .... 23, 67
   1:2 .... 45, 74
   1:3 .... 47, 50
   1:14 100
   2:14 .... 60, 69, 75
   2:15 60
   2:17 70
   3:12 194
   3:13 194
   4:2 .... 76, 198
   4:13 31
   4:15 .... 69, 75
   5:5 .... 74, 75
   5:5-7 69
   5:6 74
   5:11 133
   5:13,14 110
   6:1 234
   6:4 89
   6:5 89
   6:10 123
   6:11 .... 132, 133
   6:11,12 .... 111, 122, 134
   6:11,19 134
   6:12 .... 100, 132, 133
   6:16 167
   6:17 38
   6:17,18 .... 128, 134
   6:20 133
   7 73
   7:22 75
   7:23-25 73
   7:24 .... 69, 70
   7:25 .... 69, 70

Ending Statement, Signatories, and Appendix on Baptism

Reference	Page
7:26	69, 75
8:1-13	63
9:14	70, 76
9:15	76
9:24	76
9:25	213
9:26	213
9:28	70, 213
10:1	141
10:5	69
10:5-10	75
10:14	76, 94
10:19-21	154
10:19-39	184
10:24	183, 184, 194
10:25	163, 183, 184, 194
10:39	107
11:3	41, 43, 44
11:4,6	123
11:6	11, 31, 67
11:13	67, 110
12:1	44
12:2	44, 71, 111
12:3	71
12:6	100
12:14	104
12:23	184, 217, 222
12:25	69
13:4	177
13:8	76
13:17	186
13:21	122

James

Reference	Page
1:13	38
1:14	56, 60, 82
1:15	56, 60
1:17	27
1:25	198
2:8	141
2:10	141
2:10-12	141
2:11	141
2:14-26	119, 120
2:17	94, 120
2:18,22	122
2:22	94
2:26	94
4:1-12	153
4:12	152, 153, 154
5:12	167, 168
5:33-37	168

1 Peter

Reference	Page
1:2	39, 95
1:5	39, 125
1:10	76
1:11	76
1:18	94
1:19	74, 94
1:20	74
2:1,2	198
2:2	110
2:5	123, 181
2:7	52
2:8	52
2:11	104
2:13	172
2:15	122
2:17	169, 172, 173
3:8-13	142
3:18	75
3:19	218, 222
3:21	198
3:22	172
4:10,11	186
5:7	100

2 Peter

Reference	Page
1:1	111
1:3-11	131
1:4,5,10,11	134
1:5-11	122
1:10	39
1:10-12	70
1:19	23
1:19-21	24
1:20	23
1:20,21	25
2:4	76
2:18,21	154
3:16	24

1 John

Reference	Page
1:1-4	192
1:2	192
1:3	192, 193
1:5	38
1:7	95
1:8	60
1:9	95
2:3	134
2:3,5	122
2:16	51
2:19	128
2:20,27	24
2:24	89
2:25	89
2:28	59
3:1	97
3:1-3	134
3:25	9, 217
3:35	9
3:4	55, 58, 59
3:9	128, 134
3:10	59
3:14	134
3:17	193
3:18	193
4:1	187

4:13	134
4:18	154
5:4,5	111
5:6–21	132
5:7	32
5:9	24
5:12	132
5:13	125, 132, 134
5:14	162
5:16	162
5:20	77

2 John
1:1-4	242

3 John
1:8-10	187

Jude
1:4	39
1:6	222
1:7	218, 222
6	227

Revelation
1:3	20, 227
1:9	227
1:10	163
2	184
3	184
3:12	100
4:8	27
5:12-14	31
12:17	185
13:8	76, 147
15:4	27
18:2	184
19:10	162
22:6-21	227
22:20	226, 227, 228

www.ingramcontent.com/pod-product-compliance
Lightning Source LLC
Chambersburg PA
CBHW042357070526
44585CB00029B/2967